PEAK
Place-Names

LOUIS MCMEEKEN

HALSGROVE

First published by Halsgrove in 2003

Text copyright © 2003 Louis McMeeken

British Library Cataloguing-in-Publication Data
A CIP record for this title is available from the British Library

ISBN 1 84114 271 9

HALSGROVE
Halsgrove House
Lower Moor Way
Tiverton EX16 6SS
T: 01884 243242
F: 01884 243325
www.halsgrove.com

Printed in Great Britain by
The Cromwell Press, Trowbridge

CONTENTS

1

WHERE IS THE PEAK?

Let's briefly get this question out of the way first. The Peak District National Park was founded in 1951 as Britain's first national park, and is ostensibly that part of the Peak District which the planners decided was the most scenic and worthy of conserving. Quite obviously, places such as Buxton, Glossop and Matlock are in the wider Peak District, but they were not included within its boundaries because of their industry, particularly quarrying.

The seventh-century document known as the *Tribal Hidage* mentions Pecsaetna Lond, that is to say 'the land of the settlers of the Peak'. The next mention was the early-tenth-century *Anglo-Saxon Chronicle* which refers to Peac Lond, peac being the Old English word for a hill or peak.

Many residents nearly burst a blood vessel when people, such as weather forecasters, refer to 'the Peaks' (plural) of Derbyshire. Because really, there are few 'peaks', in the usual dictionary sense of a sharply-pointed hill, in the region and in that way the name can easily mislead visitors to the area. So it really means the 'hilly land'.

Perhaps it could be argued that there are two Peaks, the White Peak, that is the predominately limestone southern part, and the Dark, or High, Peak, which is the gritstone part lying to the north, east and west. And, of course, there is much more to the Peak District than Derbyshire – the area also covers parts of Staffordshire, Cheshire, what used to be Lancashire, and Yorkshire.

2
WHAT'S IN A NAME?

One of the easiest ways to identify a place is to mention who lives there – the village where Bert lives, or Harry's farm, and so on. And this is precisely how many settlements and even dwellings in the Peak originally gained their names.

We know very little or nothing of most of these people now, although we do know the names that were used. And they are mostly Anglo-Saxon.

Despite the assertion that Tideswell was named after an ebbing and flowing well, which can still be seen in the garden of a house in the village (although it hasn't ebbed or flowed in living memory), it was actually called after someone named Tidi. It was Tidi's stream or spring, and he was almost certainly buried at nearby Tideslow.

Well before the Scandinavian pop group appeared, the good well-watered land in moorland belonging to Abba became known as Abney. Aelle's remote valley eventually became Alsop en le Dale; while Aelfstan's open land is now known as Alstonefield – with or without the middle 'e'.

Bakewell has nothing to do with the excellence of its culinary delight, but merely tells us that Badeca considered the spring there to be his property; and the burial mound, or low, at Baslow is the resting place of Bassa. He might well have known Bega, whose clearing gives us Beeley; Bonsall could have been the steep little valley where a chap called Bunt lived, we don't really know, or it might be the place where buntings (birds) were plentiful.

A similar puzzle is Snitterton, which could be Snytra's farm, or was it named after the snipe which were once know as snitters? Other farms bearing the names of people include Brassington (personal name Brandsige), Elton (Ella), Kniveton (Cengifu), probably Offerton (Offhere?), Ogston (Oggod), Taddington (Tada), Tissington (Tidsige), and Wessington (Wigstan).

Many place-names tell us to whom the enclosure, or 'worth' belonged. These include Ceatt (Chatsworth), Cissa (Chisworth), Tet (Tittesworth), Wyrc (Wirksworth), and Bucg at Bugsworth. Bugsworth is now known as Buxworth, (except for area around the canal basin), a cosmetic name change instigated by a local schoolteacher and the vicar and made in the 1930s. A recent referendum of villagers in the hope of changing it back to its ancient original was not successful.

In the nineteenth century, the hamlets of Higher and Lower Bibbington were created for the workers at Perseverance Quarry by the owners, the Bibbington family. Carl's (or was it Charles's?) work or fortification is familiar to us as Carl Wark; Curbar is thought to mean Corda's fortified place, and Pil built his fort at Pilsbury, in the Upper Dove Valley.

A few relatively important men had hills named after them; these include Ceolmaer (Chelmorton), Hynci (Hanson Grange), Heorot (Hartington) – although this could mean hart's hill – Lang (Longstone), Scyttel (Shutlingsloe), Wineca (Wincle), and Wyrma (Wormhill). There are some, particularly those with a New Age bent, who will tell you that Wormhill means the hill of the dragon, and it is certainly true that many 'worm' place-names do indeed derive from 'wrym' meaning dragon, but in this particular instance, it doesn't seem to be the case.

Caet's thorn became Castern, Ceol's narrow and steep little valley became Chunal. It's possible, although no one is sure, that Cronkston means 'Crannuc's hill', the other theory is that it means 'heron's hill'. Bubba's hill became Bubnell, Haca's corner of land evolved into Hackney, Winster is possibly Wine's thorn bush, and Tan's clearing is a probable source of Tansley. In the Glossop area Simund had land at Simmondley, and Padda's open land became Padfield, although Padfield could equally be interpreted as 'toads' field'.

In more recent times G.H.B. 'Bert' Ward had the summit of Lose Hill named after him – 'Ward's Piece'. Bert Ward was the founder, secretary, and treasurer of the Sheffield Clarion Ramblers, as well as being the first chairman of what was to become the Ramblers' Association. The land was presented to him in 1945 in recognition of his sterling pioneer work for walkers, and he promptly passed it on to the National Trust for safekeeping. G.H.B. died in 1957, aged eighty-one.

Cruda had a cottage which is remembered by Crowdecote, and it is possible that Wulfstan had one at Wolfscote. Aedel might have had a 'place' at Eddlestow, alternatively it could simply mean 'splendid place'.

Various other folk owned or lived in valleys, including Ceof (Chee Dale), Glot (Glossop), Maessa (possibly Masson), Tatuc (Taxal), Morwine (Monsal), and once again we have a name which can be interpreted in two ways at Hassop. Is it

'Haett's valley', or does it mean the 'valley of the witches'? If we take 'ley' to mean a clearing in an old wildwood area, then the following folks were to be found there – Pil (Pilsley and Pilsbury), Ranc (Ronksley), Hroowulf or Hrolfr (Rowsley – the first element of this village name is pronounced row as in fish eggs, not row as in argument); and Wicga (Wigley). Wicga, or someone with a similar name, also had a stream (Wigwell); Grim's stream became Grindsbrook, although we don't know if he was a person, a god (Woden), or the Devil. Similarly Ecclesbourne could be 'Eccel's stream' or it could mean the stream by the church.

We know that Eccel had a 'settlement' at Ecton, Ealac had one at Elkstone, and Eadlac gave his name to Ellastone. Eadwine, or Edwin, gave his name to Eden Tree in Bradwell, and it is commonly said that King Edwin was hanged here. The facts, however, don't quite fit this story. Eadwine/Edwin king of Northumbria lived from 585 to 633 but as he was defeated and slain in battle with Penda of Mercia at Hatfield Chase, this tale does not have any credibility.

Eadin's sloping bank became Edensor, (pronounced 'Enser') although there is only one house left on the original village site, as it was razed to the ground by the Duke of Devonshire and rebuilt nearby. Penistone is believed to have derived from 'the estate near a hill called Penning'. Higgenholes means the hollows belonging to Higgens, which in some long-winded way derives from Richard, while Ibba's hollow survives as Ible. Incidentally, Ible is pronounced to rhyme with Bible.

George Fox had a shepherd's bothy or hut near Longshaw which was no doubt a well-known landmark in an otherwise uninhabited landscape, and it was this building which gave its name to the Fox House public house, which was built nearby at a later date. Many people wonder how Whatstandwell came about, and there are many fanciful stories about 'what stands well'. However, the most plausible explanation is that it derives from one Walter 'Wat' Stonewell, who owned the land on which a bridge was built over the River Derwent.

To tidy up some other people who left their names, we have Wada's ledge or plateau (Wadshelf); Pica's hall (Pikehall); Martin's slope or bank (Martinside); Kettil's island (Kettleshulme), Ipstones probably means Ippa's stones, and Hucca's burial mound gives us Hucklow.

It is not clear whether Thorncliffe, previously Thorntileg, is Thoni's slope or if it refers to a clearing among the thorn trees. Another poser is Youlgreave, which has a number of different interpretations, one of them being Geola's grove. It is popularly said that Wigginstall got its name from a wagon that stalled or became stuck in the mud, whereas it was really Wicga's cattle shippon. Finally, it is claimed that William Clough on Kinder Scout recalls a medieval miner and smelter, William the Smith, who worked hereabouts. And Alice Head might well be connected with Alice Booth, the leading Quaker at nearby Peasunhurst.

Thomas Gardom gave his name to Gardom's Edge; he was of the family who owned the original Calver Mill, and Hurts Wood in the Upper Dove belonged to the Hurt family of Castern Hall.

The steps of Jacob's Ladder on the western slopes of Kinder, which have been damaged recently to the tune of £13,000 by off-road drivers, commemorates the original steps which were cut by Jacob Marshall of Youngit Farm near Edale, to help him and his packhorses climb over the hill to Hayfield. To be precise, the bridle-way is Jacob's Ladder but the name nowadays seems to be used for the short-cut path which bypasses it. On the other hand, Jacob's Ladder in Buxton, which runs up to Hardwick Square from Terrace Road, and the Heights of Jacob in Matlock Bath, are both purely biblical allusions.

Just who Pym was, who gave his name to two Pym's Chairs, no one seems to know. One theory is that he was John Pym (1584–1643) a fiery politician who rode through England with his Scots ally Hampden urging voters to do their duty. He was also Lieutenant of the Ordnance. Other contenders include a highwayman who lurked around the Goyt Valley, and a seventeenth-century Nonconformist preacher who allegedly used the 'chair' as a pulpit. The first written evidence of the last mentioned appears to be Pim's Chayre in 1611. Doxey Pool on the Roaches was probably named after Thomas Doxey who lived at Pheasants' Clough in the seventeenth century. More recent names include Parnell Farm, where the owner admired the Irish politician Charles Stewart Parnell,

Doxey Pool on the Roaches probably named after Thomas Doxey of Pheasants' Clough

and Solomon's Hollow on the Leek to Buxton road, which was so-called after Solomon Ash who owned the land here. Another Solomon gave his name to Solomon's Temple on Grin Low. He was Solomon Mycock, the landlord of the Cheshire Cheese Inn in Buxton, who had the folly built, it is said, to employ out-of-work men. Another folly which provided work for otherwise unemployed men was Boot's Tower, on the moors near Bradfield. It was erected in 1927 by the builder Charles Boot, using stone and windows from demolished old houses.

Wellington's Monument is a stone cross erected in 1866 by Baslow's Dr E.M. Wrench. It commemorates Arthur Wellesley, Duke of Wellington, soldier and later Prime Minister, who died in 1852. Just across the valley is a 12ft-high obelisk surmounted by a stone ball, known as Nelson's Column. Close by are three large tors each incised with the names of a ship, Nelson's flagship *Victory*, Collingwood's *Soverin* (sic), and the *Defiance*. They commemorate Nelson's Napoleonic War victory over the French and Spanish fleets in the Battle of Trafalgar in 1805, during which he was fatally wounded.

Mary Queen of Scots is remembered by the name Queen Mary's Bower, a late-sixteenth-century moated gazebo in the grounds of Chatsworth, where she supposedly exercised when she was a prisoner in the charge of the Earl of Shrewsbury. Also in the Chatsworth grounds is Russian Cottage, a Russian style 'log cabin' built in 1855 from plans given to the Duke of Devonshire by Tsar Nicholas I who was due to visit. Unfortunately, he never arrived.

Commemorated by association is General Wolfe and his victory over the French at Quebec in 1759 in the fanciful name of a hill in Matlock Bath called the Heights of Abraham, now usually reached by a spectacular cable car ride.

William Peveril gave his name to the castle after which Castleton is named, and the Earl Grey Tower, built by the Thornhill family on the edge of Stanton Moor, commemorates the passing of his long-awaited Reform Bill in 1832.

Coatestown, near Hollinsclough, gained its name because three of the four families living there were called Coates. Mather's Grave, near Brackenfield, is named after Samuel Mather, a poor soul who committed suicide and, as was the custom, was buried on unconsecrated ground at a crossroads.

WOODLAND NAMES

Many woodlands bear the names of people who were instrumental in establishing them, as is shown in the following list of plantations which have taken the surname of the person mentioned:

In the Brassington area: Joseph Beardsley (i.e. Beardsley Plantation)
Darley Dale: George Clarke 1663; Mary Newton 1645 (Newtonlot)
Hopton: Henry Twigge 1610 (Twig)
Peak Forest: William Hartle 1713; Adam Jackson 1733; Thomas Watts 1617
Stanton in Peak: John Wain 1846
Tideswell: John Radford 1829
Walton: Ralph Mather 1640 (Matherbank); James Riggot 1670
Wingerworth: Ellen Simpson 1864

Similarly, the following woods have taken the name of their one-time owner:
In the Ashover area: William Outram (i.e. Outram Wood); John Sleigh 1629;
James Storrs 1780 (Stars Wood)
Barlow: Robert Allen 1562; William Harker 1829
Brackenfield: the Knowles family
Brampton: George Symes 1673 (Sims Wood)
Matlock: Anthony Goodwin 1678
Over Haddon: Lady Palmerston 1857
Stanton in Peak: Robert Bateman 1682 (Bateman Firs)
Tissington: William Bassett 1498
Winster: George White 1734
Wirksworth: Thomas & William Bunting 1577.

STRANGER THAN FICTION

During the course of the author's work as an assistant in the Bakewell Tourist
Information Centre, there is a constant trickle of enquiries for the place featured
in the television series 'League of Gentlemen', 'Royston Vasey'. Much to the
surprise of some enquirers, this is not a real village at all, but is based on Hadfield
(heathy open land). Bizarrely, it is also the real name of comedian Roy 'Chubby'
Brown.

Another imaginary place people try to find is the village of Cardale in the
popular television series 'Peak Practice'. It was originally filmed in Crich, and
latterly in Longnor.

It is constantly amazing how many people believe television soaps to be factual.
There was a flurry of enquirers in Hartington looking for the
non-existent Blackberry Lane when 'Coronation Street' character Hilda Ogden
left the series to become housekeeper to a doctor there.

∽∞∾

3

NAMES IN HIGH PLACES

This section could have been called hills and mountains, but although older books tend to speak of the mountains of the Peak District, none of the hills can truly be called mountains.

Although there is no precise definition of a mountain, it is generally accepted that to be classified as a mountain a hill has to be over 2000 feet above sea level, in which case Kinder Scout, with an altitude of 2088ft (636m), and Bleaklow, 2060ft (628m), would qualify. However, others aver that it is not just the height that matters, there must be a discernable summit too, and Kinder, being a plateau, doesn't seem to fall into this category.

Having got that out of the way, what does Kinder Scout, the highest point in the Peak District, mean? The short answer is that nobody knows. The oldest recorded name for Kinder is Chendre in 1086, which had become Kender by 1275. Ekwall suggested that it derived from coned and bre; coned probably being a personal name, with bre meaning hill. Yet another conjecture is 'place with wide views' from the Welsh word conderc. Others have suggested that Scout means 'projecting hill, or overhanging rock', from the Old Norwegian skuti.

Walking along a grough on Kinder   DEREK ABBERLEY

The only hill that can really be said to be posing as a mountain is Mount Famine near Hayfield, though the one to which most guidebooks give the designation of 'mountain' is Mam Tor. Because the shale east face is liable to crumble and fall at times, it has acquired the soubriquet, the 'Shivering Mountain', although locals are never heard to call it that. The nickname is probably due to Thomas Hobbes, who seems to have been the first to record it.

It seems that certain descriptions are invented by visitors and are repeated. Another example is Chrome and Parkhouse Hills, which no one in Hollinsclough calls the 'Dragon's Back'. The most straightforward description of a mass of rocks is the Roaches, which comes from the French and means simply 'the rocks'.

The Anglo-Saxons, and others, who were more aware of the lie of the land than modern man, had a variety of words to describe hills. No doubt they each had subtle, slightly differing meanings, which perhaps we have not yet managed to decipher.

The commonest of the terms used for humps and bumps and high masses of land in the Peak District are hill, from the Old English hyll, and low, again from an Old English word hlaw.

A low tends to be a rounded or conical hill. As is repeated *ad nauseum*, in the Peak District low usually means high. The word for a hill or tumulus is low, from the Old English hlaw, and is used for both but mainly for burial mounds. People who speak with a strong Derbyshire accent pronounce 'low' as 'la', for example Basla for Baslow, and Copla Dale for Coplow Dale.

Here are some of the 'low' place-names, with the meaning of the first name element in brackets.

Arbor Low – Harberlowe 1533 (earth work); Bleaklow (dark); Calling Low (disputed – probably a boundary); Callow (bare); Dirtlow (dirty); Foolow (many coloured); Grindlow (green); Grin Low (green); Haddock Low (how intriguing!); the delightfully contradictory Highlow (high); Hindlow (deer); Hucklow (personal name Hucca); Hurdlow (treasure hoard); Merryton Low (could be' enclosed marsh', but far more likely to be 'burial place by boundary land'); Mich Low (from micel meaning big or great); Moat Low (an assembly of people, a meeting place, a court) , this word 'moat' is related to moot, or mote, and was a meeting place for the Wapentake. 'Mote' is still found in the Barmote Court, from bargh (mining) plus mote; Rowlow (rough); Shutlingsloe (personal name Scyttel); Slipperlow (having a smooth, slippery surface); Sparklow (covered with shrubs); Tideslow (personal name Tidi); Wardlow (lookout); Warslow (probably the same as Wardlow, but could be the personal name Wer).

In addition to these we have other terms for high ground. A knoll is a lump or knob, and is usually used for the summit of a hill; there is a Moisty (damp) Knoll in Stoney Middleton, and a Rebellion Knoll in Bradwell. Quite which rebellion gave this knoll its name is another mystery waiting to be solved.

Tor is applied to a rocky outcrop or height such as Mam Tor or Shining Tor. Shining is a strange adjective for a landscape feature, which has variously been interpreted literally as shining, glittering, or bright and as having an allusion to ghosts or spirits. Jeal Torrs in Tideswell is from the Gaelic word for white – geal. Drabber Tor is 'dull coloured', and Higger Tor is 'higher', presumably higher than the surrounding outcrops.

A cop can be defined as the top of a hill, a summit or mound, but it does seem that cops are particularly hills with a narrow summit, like Wardlow Cop. Fin Cop could take its name from the Celtic word for white or clear, which is 'fin'.

Cruc or cryc is Old Welsh for a hill or mound, and this is why Crook Hill is so -called, later folk not realising that Crook meant hill added another Hill making it 'hill hill!' Crich also developed from this root.

Mam Tor is variously said to mean Mother Hill – with her arms around Edale and the Hope Valley, or more likely 'the round shaped hill'; both from Celtic words for either mother or breast. The Knot at Hayfield simply means rocky hill.

When borough is encountered in a name it is a mound or fort, as can be gib, from Middle English gibbe meaning a hump. Above Glossop is Cock Hill, and probably this derived from the Old English cocc meaning a hillock, however it could be argued that it had something to do with male fowl. A hillock is of course a small hill; White Hillocks in Ashover gain their description from the whiteness produced by its crystals of calcite.

Den, don and dun all mean hill, or an open upland area; the latest thinking tends towards dun being a flat shelf-like tract of land with higher land above it. A good example is Chelmorton (Chelmerdon in 1108) which nestles 250 feet below Chelmorton Low. Other places including the dun/don suffix include Sheldon (either heath hill, or possibly village on a shelf of a hill), Grindon (green hill), Staden (stave hill), Haddon (heath hill), Bowden (curved hill), Hanson (Hynci's hill – Hanzedone 1086), and Hartington (either Heorot's hill or hart's hill – Hartedun in 1086).

The confusing thing about 'den' in place-names is that it can also mean the exact opposite of a hill – a valley. Yet another meaning is a woodland pasture, so great care is needed when determining which should apply to a particular place. Gun Hill is popularly so-called because Oliver Cromwell's men are said to have fired a cannon from here at Leek. However, in the previous century it was recorded as Dunne, so perhaps Dunne, became Dun and then Gun. In other words, Hill was added to a word (dun) meaning 'hill', so it became another 'hill hill'.

Pike derives from the Old English pic, a spike, and is applied to hills with a sharp point or summit; Topley Pike means pointed rocky hill. A cliff can be defined as a slope with an incline that is more perpendicular than horizontal, and a scar a rocky outcrop with a steep face.

Lesser slopes are yeld, yelt, heald and hield; whereas when side is used in a name it suggests a long hill. The word 'hanging' is frequently found on the map, and, naturally enough, people make the assumption that this was where there used to be gallows. I suppose it's always possible, but the accepted meaning is a land on a steep slope. Examples are Hanging Bridge and Hanging Holes, in the Darley Dale area. A low bank used as a boundary is called either a bang, bonk, or bong, although these terms equally apply to a slope in an otherwise flat area. Hilum was the name Ilam (pronounced eye-lam) had in 1004, and would seem to be a variation of hyll, the Old English word for a hill. Perhaps it simply means the settlement in the hills.

Bosley Minn and Wincle Minn employ a Celtic word for a brink or edge, an edge usually being a dramatic escarpment terminating in a plateau. Ridge can be defined as a long narrow stretch of ground, but where the suffix 'over' is found it denotes a flat-topped ridge with a rounded shoulder. Saddleworth is 'the enclosure on a saddle-shaped ridge'. Three names with roughly similar meanings are Nab and The Nabs – a rocky projection or promontory; naze – a nose or promontory; and head – a projecting point of rock or an extremity. Teggs Nose is promontory inhabited by teggs; we think of a teg as a two-year- old sheep, but it was also used as a word for a female deer.

Rowtor, as in Rowtor Rocks, and Rowter Farm, means 'rough rock'; in this case it is millstone grit. The same meaning is found in the village name Rowarth, 'rough enclosure'. Knarrs, as found at Hayfield, and Tintwistle Knarr, signifies a 'rugged rock', whilst Kerridge is a 'boulder ridge' from caeg, hrycg. Laddow Rocks might come from ladda meaning servant or lad, or possibly from the Old Norse word lad meaning a heap or pile. Rainster Rocks belonged to Isaac Raines in the eighteenth century, and the nearby Pinder's Rock was on the property of Jane Pindar about the same time.

Now let's look at some hill names and give the meaning of the name. Wind Low, Windy Knowl, and Windgather Rocks, 'the gather wynd' in 1611, speak for themselves, and they are indeed well named. A knowl(e) is a hillock. Below Windy Knowl, the Winnats Pass is a contraction of the wind-gates. A surprising hill name is Holymoorside, but in 1584 it was called Howley Moor, the first part meaning hill clearing, gradually being corrupted to Holy.

A cycle race in the Winnats, or 'wind gates' Pass

Haven Hill at Bradbourne was previously recorded as 'heaven hill'. Another place with a seeming heavenly connection is Steeple Grange in Wirksworth, but this steeple was known as Stephul in 1230 and Steephill in 1630. Spellor Ground near Brassington must have been a site of some importance because it translates as the 'hill where the speeches are made'. Merrill is the 'hill with good pasturage', but nearby Elton, and Tissington, both have a Hunger Hill where the tenant would not live on the fat of the land.

So far nobody has explained High Wheeldon's name; it is generally supposed to mean 'wheel hill', but why should it be called that? It has been put forward that there might have been a stone circle or a (mill) wheel here but it's all a bit airy-fairy. This hill, standing at 1385 feet, has magnificent 360° views from the top, and was given as a memorial to the men of the Derbyshire and Staffordshire who fell in the two world wars.

Nearby Chrome Hill is pronounced 'croom' by locals, and older maps spell it that way. It comes from crum, meaning crooked or bent, and it is plain to see

The curve of Chrome Hill which gave it its name

why with its lovely curved back. This same root is to be found in the name Cromford, which is 'the ford on the bend' (of the River Derwent); in fact, many Derbyshire people pronounce it Crumford.

Some hills straightforwardly are given the name of the one-time owner. Andrew's Knob, Bagshaw Hill, and Eaton Hill, are all family names. Goosehill in Castleton might relate to the bird, or probably to the de Gosehill family who lived here in medieval times, then again were the family named after the hill? As already stated, an interest in place-names is a fascinating study, but it is so very easy to get things askew.

There is an interesting local name for the road from Wardlow towards Monsal Head – 'Scratter'. Scrat is a dialect word meaning to scratch or claw, and I am told that the name came about because horses had to 'scrat' up the long hill. However, the standard explanation is that it comes from skratti meaning a demon or devil.

The rocky eminence above Ashover is known as The Fabric. Local legend has it that the stone, or fabric, for the church was quarried here. What is recorded is that Leonard Wheatcroft, one-time parish clerk, built Fabrick House 'upon the top of Ashover Hill' in 1691 – fabrick meaning 'building'.

Lantern Pike would once have had a beacon on top, as was common across the nation for warnings and other communications. Both Blore and Mellor are village names meaning 'bare hill', although as is so often the case another interpretation can be given to Blore, that of 'a windy place'.

Parkhouse Hill in the Upper Dove valley would be the hill near the house in the deer park, presumably Glutton Grange. One of the nearby hillocks or pinnacles of rock is called Sugar Loaf, and this harks back to the days when sugar came in an unrefined hard mass that was roughly conical in shape. Across the road is Hitter Hill, and the only explanation seen by the author for that is 'the hill owned by the blacksmith', though it is not very convincing. If there was a hill which gave a good vantage point over the surrounding countryside it was described as a Toot Hill. Blue Hills in the Roaches syncline in Staffordshire are thought to be so-named because of the coal deposits there, while Pet Hills probably uses the old word for a pit meaning a hole or quarry.

Bank, bonk, and side, as stated above, can all mean a slope or hillside. Longwaybank, between Whatstandwell and Wirksworth, is the long hill spur, and Gypsy Bank is the hillside where gipsies grazed their horses when they had a gathering at Coldeaton crossroads. Phoside has the same meaning (and root word) as Foolow, which is 'many coloured hillside'. Yokecliffe at Wirksworth has a singular colour, yellow; perhaps before the housing estate was erected the slope was covered in gorse or broom.

The name of the small village of Oker (or is it Oaker?) means 'hill of conflict', and derives from the Latin *occurus*. What the conflict was, and whether it involved Romans, we shall never know.

When 'over' or 'or' is found in a name it can signify a high ridge, so Longnor would be 'the long, high ridge' (a good topographical description of the hilltop village between the Dove and Manifold valleys), and Birchover the 'birch trees on the high ridge'. Langsett has a similar meaning of long hill or slope, from 'side'. Black Hill is occasionally called Soldiers' Lump; this came about when the Royal Engineers used the hill as a triangulation station in 1784.

'Edge' is not the most difficult concept to grasp, being the edge of high ground, usually with an accompanying steep cliff. The Eastern Edges are about 25 miles long and the edge changes its name every so often, sometimes to the name of the settlement beneath, such as Baslow, Curbar, and Froggatt. Stanage is simply the 'stone edge', Cown Edge is above the river (Sett), being derived from what is assumed to be an earlier name for the Sett, the Colun. Morridge is the 'moor edge', and what a beautiful drive it is on the road which follows this edge, especially in late summer when the heather is in bloom.

18

4

DALES, DIMPLES AND DELLS

The word 'valley', derived from Old French for an elongated hollow between hills, is common enough in the Peak District, but it is easily outnumbered by the vast number of its Old Norse equivalent 'dalr' or 'dale'. There is a subtle, and not yet fully understood, difference between all the different terms for these dents in the landscape, and here is some attempt to impart what they represent.

Possibly the smallest 'dent' or hollow would be called a hole, which is probably not much different to a dimple or dumpel, being closely followed by a nook, which is a secluded, sheltered place, often triangular in shape. A hollow in this context seems to be a shallow dale, and 'slack' has a roughly similar meaning. Hollow comes from the Old English 'halh' which is found as part of the names of such as Chunal, Monsal, and Bonsall.

A dell or delf can be described as a tiny valley; usually well wooded or with an abundance of foliage, it comes from the Old English word, (ge)delf, meaning a quarry, so close examination may reveal evidence of earlier digging. While a can(n) is a steep-sided valley, a clough would fit the same description, although invariably with a stream flowing through it.

Two examples are Roych Clough (stony), Leyzing Clough, which has the interesting meaning of 'freed man's clough', and Wildboarclough. There are two places with this last mentioned name and both are said to be the place where the last wild boar in the Peak District was killed. There must be a slight difference between a clough and a dumble, which too is a ravine containing a stream, or alternatively, a wooded valley.

The jury is still out on quite what hop, or hope, means. Some say a hop is a side valley, whilst most toponymists argue that it means 'a small remote enclosed valley', even a blind valley. It occurs in place-names in Hope; Stanshope (stony), and as '-op' in names such as Glossop; Hassop – Haett's valley; Bradnop – broad valley; Hopton – remote valley settlement; Ashopton – farm in the ash tree valley; Sydnope – probably broad valley. 'Hope' can appear in names as the suffix 'up', like Rushup which is the 'rush valley', Rushup Edge being the edge above it. The root word 'denu' appears to be a long, sinuous, main valley. An example would be Longdendale, which is tautological being 'long, valley, valley'. Coomb, comb, and cumb are shorter, broader dales than these and are usually basin-shaped with three fairly steep hilly sides. There is a village called Combs, which most people call 'coombs', although some locals call it carms and combs, pronounced like the toothed implement used to groom hair. Bottom is the name given to wide valleys containing a river.

Walkers descending into unimaginative, but appropriately named Deep Dale, near King Sterndale   DEREK ABBERLEY

It seems worth listing the many dales for the curious reader, so here they are, with an occasional meaning.

AN A–Z OF DALES

Alport Dale; Ashwood Dale; Back Dale; Backwood Dale; Bagshaw Dale; Bakestone Dale; Beresford Dale; Biggin Dale; Blackwell Dale; Bonsall Dale; Bradfield Dale; Bradford Dale; Bradwell Dale; Bramley Dale – place where the broom grows; Brierlow Dale – near the hill covered in briars, or brambles; Bullhay Dale; Cales Dale; Calling Low Dale; Cave Dale – supposedly formed as a dale when the roof of a cavern fell in; Channon Dale; Chee Dale; Conies Dale; Coombs Dale; Coplow Dale; Cow Dale; Cressbrook Dale; Cunning Dale; Dale of Goyt – now known as the Goyt Valley (the original name for the hardy Gritstone sheep first bred here was Dale o' Goyt); Dam Dale – gains its name from an old dam forming the 'great pond of Peak Forest'; Darley Dale – a name said to have been invented by the Reverend Daniel Vawdry, or the railway company, to encompass the hamlets of Churchtown, Hackney, Hillside and Northwood; Deep Dale – two of this name; Demon Dale; Derwent Dale; Dimmins Dale – demons' dale; Dovedale; Doveholes Dale; Dowel Dale – possibly Dove spring; Dry Dale; Eaton Dale; Edale – this is the name of the valley (the etymology is uncertain but it probably means patches, or islands, of good land in a moorland area; Edale village is properly Grindsbrook Booth); Eyam Dale; Fernydale; Flag Dale; Flax Dale; Glossopdale; Glutton Dale; Gratton Dale; Great Rocks Dale – this was Greteraches in 1251, meaning great valleys (there is a main dale with a number of small dales leading off); Green Dale – three of these, and no sign of Postman Pat!; Hall Dale – two of this name, the one at Alstonefield was previously called Stanshope; Hand Dale; Hartington Dale; Hartle Dale; Havenhill Dale; Hay Dale – two of this name; High Dale; Hipley Dale; Hope Dale – not to be confused with Hope Valley, this one is near Alstonefield; Horse Dale; Horseshoe Dale – from the shape; Hubber Dale; Intake Dale; Jennings Dale; Kidtor Dale; Killer Dale – Killer is a local surname in Wirksworth; Kirk Dale; Lathkill Dale – apparently means narrow dale with a barn; Lin Dale; Linen Dale; Litton Dale; Lomberdale – boundary valley; Long Dale – two of this name; Longdendale – literally long valley valley; Lumsdale;

The tradition goes on – a modern boundary marker in Long Dale, defining the edge of the parish of Middleton and Smerrill

Waterfall in Monsal Dale

Madge Dale – Mag's valley; Matlock Dale; Megdale; Middleton Dale; Mill Dale; Millers Dale; Monks Dale – once owned by Lenton Abbey in Nottinghamshire, which was founded by William Peveril (there is no substance to the story of a tunnel running from here to 'a monastery' in Tideswell); Monsal Dale; Nabs Dale; Narrowdale – there is an expression 'keep it for the Narrowdale sun', meaning to put it off indefinitely (according to Brewer's *Dictionary of Phrase and Fable,* when the sun's rays first pierce the dale in spring, it is only for a few minutes in the afternoon); Nettler Dale; Northern Dale; Over Dale; Peak Dale; Perry Dale – where the pears grew; Peter Dale; Pindale; Ravensdale; Ricklow Dale; Roller Dale – by rough hill (Rowlow); Sandy Dale – not shown on maps, but described in James Croston's *On Foot Through The Peak* as leading from Millers Dale to Taddington; Sharplow Dale; Silly Dale – despite it being near the seemingly apposite Foolow it means happy, prosperous valley; Smalldale – two of this name; Stanlow Dale – 'stone hill dale'; Sterndale – 'stony dale', prefixed by both King's and Earl (of Derby); Sydnope Dale; Taddington Dale; Tansley Dale – a transferred name, this is near Litton; Tideswell Dale; Two Dales – formerly Toadhole; Upper Dale; Water-cum-Jolly Dale – this is one which no one really knows, but everyone and his wife wants to know (it could be 'water with a pretty valley', or possibly 'water with a fat, or large, valley'); Wensley Dale; Wolfscote Dale; Wigger Dale; Woo Dale – wolves dale; Wye Dale.

The delightful, but puzzlingly named, Water-cum-Jolly Dale

5
RIVERS, STREAMS AND OTHER WET PLACES

The rivers of the Peak are different from the vast majority of other place-names in that they retain names which could be unchanged since they were first named by the first prehistoric settlers. Some, such as the Churnet and Amber, have names that defy explanation, although it is said the Amber takes its name from the colour, but this seems a very weak interpretation.

The Celtic word 'dubh' means black (as in Dublin which means black pool), and this is believed to be the description of the River Dove. Dove Holes near Buxton, however, probably gets its name a dialect form of dive or dived, referring to the holes where the water fell or took a dive underground. Dove Head, like other 'heads', is the source, or head, of the river. Similarly Wye Head is (one of) the source(s) of the Wye, which is the 'moving one' or 'carrier'; this river flows to join the Derwent at Rowsley.

At one time the Derwent was notable for its trees, as it is 'abounding in oaks' (derva meaning oak). Although it sounds warlike, Axe Edge derives from the Celtic word 'isca' meaning water, still found in the Scots words for whisky – uisque beatha or water of life. This is very apt and apparent when one considers that it is from this vicinity that all the following rivers rise: Dove, Dane, Wye, Manifold, Goyt and thus ultimately the Mersey.

Goyt, goit, and gote all mean a channel or watercourse, in fact, some people call a mill-stream powering the wheel at a mill a goyt, although probably most would call it a leat.

The Manifold is quite simply the river with many folds or bends. Another winding river in the Staffordshire moorlands is the Hamps – and 'winding' could be what 'hamps' means. Another school of thought suggests the alternative 'summer-dry', which fits equally well as in the dry weather it flows underground, occasionally re-emerging.

There is no connection between the people of Denmark and the River Dane, which has variously been interpreted as 'trickle' and 'slow-moving stream'. Yet another explanation is that the name comes from the Celtic water god

Danu or Dana. The proponents of this theory point out that the infant Dane flows very near to Lud Church and Lud was a Celtic sky god who was married to Dana.

Leek is an interesting case of a town being named after a small brook (Old English 'lece'), thought to be the spout or stream which ran down Edward Street from the vicinity of the parish church. Not so long ago Edward Street was known as Spout Street, and there is still a Spout Hall there. The stream in Parwich doesn't appear to be named – it is conjectured that it was called the Pevre Brook, and it is thought that the village name means farm by this river; it was Pevrewic in the Domesday Book.

One of the Anglo-Saxon words for a brook was burna (giving rise to the Scottish 'burn'). This developed into 'bourne' so we have Ashbourne (brook by the ash tree), Ecclesbourne (Eccel's brook or feasibly stream by a church), and Bradbourne (broad brook). Broc was also the word for a brook; often a brook takes the name of a nearby settlement, others are in some way descriptive of it such as Cressbrook (where cress is found); Meerbrook (boundary brook); Lockerbrook (by an enclosure); Wyming Brook (circuitous, zigzagging); Bletch Brook (black); Fair Brook (fair as in clear, beautiful); Rymas Brook (flowing through pasture on a bank); Mere Brook (boundary); Scow Brook (probably, in a hollow); Wash Brook (sheep washing), and Black Leach Brook (black, boggy). In the last example the word leach makes the name tautological, as it means 'stream running through boggy land'.

The most obvious clue to a settlement having a watercourse running through it is the suffix 'ford'. To name but a few, giving the name of the first element – Ashford (ash tree); Bamford (beam, who knows whether it was a plank or tree?); Beresford (beavers'); Bradford (broad); Hollowford (running in a hollow); Grindleford (probably, grinding mill, and it has also been suggested that there were stepping stones made of grindles, or grindstones); Lumford (most likely 'by a pool', but just conceivably 'in a wooded valley'), and of course there is the village simply called Ford. We think of Quarnford as being an area, but the original 'Querneford', meaning 'ford by the mill', was situated on the River Dane near Gradbach.

Tiny watercourses with names originating from the Old English 'sic' (small stream) include sitch, sytch, such, sich, sick, sike, and seech. The Anglo-Saxons also had the words rith and rithing for small streams, these becoming reth, redy and ready. Yet another name for a stream, or sometimes a stream-valley, was bache or batch, as in Gradbach.

Osiers, a species of willow especially suitable for basket weaving, grew by the River Hipper, the latter being a dialect word for this tree which comes from the Old English 'hyper'. Henmore means 'marshy ground frequented by moorhens', brook having been added at a later date.

There are two Bentley Brooks; the one which flows into the Dove takes its name from the village of Fenny Bentley, whereas the one in the Matlock area was previously called Kyrkbrook (1417) after the nearby parish church or kirk. Grain derives from an Old Norse word 'greine', meaning a fork, and usually signifies a fork in a stream (Grains in the Water on Bleaklow) although sometimes it is used to denote a small valley forking off another. Grinah Stones, also on Bleaklow, is recorded as Graine Well Stones in 1627, which is 'the boulders by the spring at the fork in the stream'. Geologically speaking, a stone isn't a boulder, but in the vernacular there is very little difference. Another word for a river fork is 'twizle', and this can be found in Tintwistle although scholars can't agree what the first part of this place-name means.

The Dunge Brook flowed through well-manured land, and the derivation is pretty obvious. The River Noe which tumbles down from Kinder means 'flow' and the stream that joins it at Hope, Peakshole Water, is what it says – water from Peak Hole, a former name for 'The Devil's Arse' or Peak Cavern.

The Etherow is a strange name which is thought to mean 'watercourse by a projecting ridge of land'.

Water, and its effects, plays a great part in Peak District names. It is not at all obvious that Mytham Bridge is an indication of water, except the possibility of the bridge spanning a canal or river, but it becomes clear once we realise that Mytham comes from an Old English word meaning the joining of two rivers – this is where the Derwent and Noe combine. There are 'wells' aplenty, 'well' in most cases meaning spring/stream rather than the type that Pussy fell down; examples are Cordwell (cold-) and Bradwell (broad-). When 'wall' appears in place-names the chances are that it is a well or spring, for example in Hargatewall.

From the same root as lece (brook) come the names lache, leash, and leche meaning a pond, quagmire, or marshy stream, giving us Wythen Lache (willows), The Laches, Leash Fen, Rewlach (rough, boggy area) and Readyleach (reedy). Still on boggy ground, there is Miry Clough, Red (reed) Mires, and Wardlow Mires.

Two places are called Strines, which is simply Middle English (strind) for a watercourse. Unsurprisingly, Wetton is the 'wet hill', and Waterfall is a bit of a puzzle but probably refers to the place that the River Hamps 'falls' underground at nearby Waterhouses. Quarters Farm near Bradwell is thought to be a corruption of waters. The exact location of the place called Watrefeld (water field) recorded in the Domesday Book is not known but because of this name, and the nearby Nether Water Farm, is thought to be in this vicinity.

Wash is marked on some maps, indeed there is a hamlet of that name, meaning what it says, be it a place for industrial washing or a sheepwash. On larger-scale maps, sheepwashes are indicated and the ones in the Peak are at Ashford-in-the-Water, a particularly fine example of a sheepwash bridge with attached pen, a demonstration is sometimes held in June; Lumford at Bakewell; northwest of Hollinsclough below Leycote; a splendid example on the River Bradford at Middleton-by-Youlgreave, often mistaken for industrial remains; near Coldwall Bridge on the River Dove, and northwest of Tideswell on Bottom Brook.

Car(r) in a name tells us that the land is wet or boggy. A good example is the story from Hollinsclough, where there is a bog, with a bog-oak, behind Mosscar Farm. Bog-oak is much sought after by furniture makers, and Harpur-Crewe sent some men and a horse to pull it out for that purpose in order to furnish the

A demonstration of sheep-washing at Sheepwash Bridge, Ashford-in-the-Water

Sheep in the enclosure of Ashford-in-the-Water Sheepwash Bridge, ready to be washed in the River Wye

family seat at Calke Abbey. Such was the state of the ground that the horse got stuck and had to be shot, and its bones are still there – with the bog-oak!

The names Eyam (pronounced 'eem') and Edale are closely related being 'place at the island' and 'island dale' respectively. As there seems to be a singular lack of islands in these areas, one suspects that 'island' means higher or drier ground in an otherwise damp area.

Grough seems to be a word only used in the Peak, usually quoted as 'hags and groughs'. A grough is a drainage channel in peat as found on Kinder, Bleaklow and Black Hill, and a hag is the firmer, higher ground that rises from the grough.

6
IF YOU GO DOWN IN THE WOODS TODAY...

Although in 55BC Julius Caesar reported that Britain was largely covered with woodland, modern archaeological thinking believes that prehistoric Man was responsible for much clearance of the original wildwood well before that. But it is the Normans who are usually credited with creating forests.

Possibly because of our childhood memories of stories of Robin Hood and his merry men, most of us have the conception of a forest as being a very large, dense wood. The dictionary definition of a forest, though, is 'an extensive tract of unenclosed land covered with trees and undergrowth, sometimes intermingled with pasture.'

In fact, in the Middle Ages a forest was a place used by the king and some select others for hunting deer, and any other beast that could be chased; it could include moorland, scrub, wasteland, cultivated land, heath, as well as woodland. Under Forest Law, there were horrendous penalties, involving mutilation of both man and hunting dog, for poaching in these forests, although in practice it seems that a monetary fine was invariably preferred by the authorities, and no doubt by the poacher.

The local forest in this area was the Royal Forest of the Peak, which covered about 40 square miles of hunting ground bounded on the north by the River Etherow, the Derwent on the east, the Wye to the south, and the Goyt on the western side. It was a royal hunting forest, and the last monarch to hunt there was Henry III.

Sometime in the early 1500s the deer population had diminished, and it was decided to concentrate the remaining animals in an enclosed park. The ranger in charge had a house called the 'Chamber of the Forest', and gradually others built their cottages nearby, forming the nucleus of what is now Peak Forest village. There is still a Chamber Farm, La Chambre in 1383, and a Chamberknoll in Peak Forest as well as Dogmanslack Farm, the last mentioned means 'shallow valley where the dog man lived', a reference to the chap who looked after the hunting dogs.

A wood which existed before the Norman Conquest would be known to the Anglo-Saxons as a frith; Leekfrith being the frith belonging to Leek. In fact, it

28

was cleared of woodland by the monks from Dieulacres Abbey in the 1300s. Holmfirth is the clearing in the wood by Holme, the name of a river and village a few miles away. Although frith is generally accepted as meaning a wood, the latest research by toponymists suggests that a frith was probably brushwood or scrub on the edge of a forest.

Small woods went by an interesting selection of titles. A grove, greeve, or greave, was a small managed wood or thicket not normally near any other woodland. The village of Youlgr(e)ave is said by some to mean either Geola's grove or yellow grove, and one wonders what sort of trees they would be to warrant such a description. Perhaps it was named in autumn? An isolated wood on a hill was called a hurst, a wood composed of thorn trees would be a spinney, while a general term for woods of a single species would be a holt.

A common term for a small wood is a shaw or shay, as is found in Bradshaw (broad-), and Shayside. A young plantation, or brushwood, was sometimes called a spray, as in Spray House Farm. Moscar means brushwood in a boggy area; Moscar Cross was a boundary cross.

The ancient practice of coppicing, where native deciduous trees were cut down to stump level so that they would throw up vigorous new shoots in the spring which could be successively harvested again and again for 'poles', gives us the name coppice. Interestingly, coppiced trees live longer than those which are allowed to grow naturally.

Copse is the same as coppice, and where the word spring is found in the context of a wood it too shows that it was a coppice wood. But it doesn't end there. Where coppicing is done within a wood various terms were used, such as hagg, fell, cant and sale. Effectively, coppicing died out in the nineteenth century, when the advent of the railways resulted in coal replacing wood as fuel.

It is thought that Tansley means the wood from which shoots were obtained, although another possibility is 'Tan's clearing'. Houses in woods were known as Woodseats, saete being a house.

It is possible in certain cases to determine what sort of trees make up a wood by the name used for it; Lound comes from Old Norse and means a grove, or even a sacred grove. One often hears Derbyshire people talk of 'ridding' something, in other words chucking it out or otherwise disposing of it, and this same word when found on a map signifies a similar activity. It shows that trees have been grubbed out and a clearing made; other related terms are roding, reed, and royd.

Ridding shouldn't be confused with riding, or ride, which is a track through a wood. A place in the wood where trees had been felled, particularly on a slope, was also called a hagg.

Henry VIII ordered a survey of all ecclesiastical property in 1535, and his inspectors reported alleged debauchery and corruption, leading to the Dissolution of the Monasteries. Smaller monasteries were dissolved in 1536 and the others in 1541, lands being taken by the Crown. Therefore, any woods containing references to the inhabitants of these establishments and their granges can safely be assumed to be prior (no pun intended) to these dates.

Examples are Monks Wood, Nunswood, and Priors Wood. Mincing Wood comes from the Anglo-Saxon, and has nothing to do with walking with affected nicety or chopping into fine pieces, but derives from minchen which is a feminine form of monk. The earlier name of Fearfall Wood in Hope was Frierwall, meaning 'friar well'. Kiss Wood in Wincle was previously called Kiss Arse Wood and no doubt the Victorians cleaned the name up – however, it comes from kjoss and ears and simply means the hill and wood in a hollow. More recent woodlands are given names such as plantation, furze, firs, and cover.

Old pigsties at the former monastic farm, One Ash Grange

Let's take a look at the many types of tree to be found in the Peak District. Alders thrive in wet land so it is no surprise to find Alderwasley meaning 'the alders that grow in the clearing near the alluvial land'. Ollerbrook was the stream with alders along its banks, and Ollerenshaw was the alder grove. A wood composed of alders often takes the name carr. It doesn't need a Sherlock Holmes to deduce that 'the ford by the ash tree' is Ashford, and 'the ash tree by the clear stream' is the meaning of Ashbourne, Ashop is the 'ash tree valley' and 'the flat-topped ridge with an ash tree' denotes Ashover. While Monyash had according to its name many ashes, the nearby grange was distinguished by having just one – One Ash Grange.

Mapleton, some times spelt Mappleton, had many trees of the type *Acer campestre* which can be found in garden centres, more commonly known as field maple. Oddly enough, lyme, as in Lyme Park near Stockport, is not the same as lime, but comes from an old word for a forest. We would usually refer to the bush that bears the sloe berry as a blackthorn, but the name Slaley means the clearing where the sloe tree grows.

The thorn was often used as a waymarker, particularly at a meeting of ways. Being extremely hardy, it can attain a height of 20ft if left to grow unhindered. We don't know what fruit was grown in the various places with orchard in their name, but Perryfoot comes from the word for a pear.

On the other hand 'the flat-topped ridge with birch trees' became Birchover, while 'the ravine with birch trees' was Birchin Clough, Birchinlee tells us that there was a forest clearing with birches. Freebirch in Brampton is listed in *White's Directory* of 1857 as Threebirch, and before that was called Trebirches.

The River Derwent was apparently 'abounding in oaks' as that is apparently what its Celtic name means, and the explicit 'death oak' or place where criminals were hanged is Dethick. More oaks were found on the ridge at Okeover, and on the moor at Oakamoor, while, appropriately, Matlock, still the administrative centre of the county of Derbyshire, was the 'council meeting place by the oak'.

Places with withen or wither in them allude to the willow tree, and the bog with the willows sounds much better to our ears as Wythen Lache. Win Hill also means the hill with willows, as it was recorded in the thirteenth century as Wythinehull.

It is a generally known fact that Hollin in a place-name means holly, and holly bushes were used as boundary markers. It was also grown as winter fodder for animals. It follows that Hollinsclough is the clough where the holly grew – it's obvious isn't it? Wrong! If we look at the spelling of the place in 1390 we see that it was Howelsclough, suggesting a hollow way, so it is thought that Hollinsclough is the valley through which the 'road' went. Spire Hollins in Glossop was in all probability mature holly trees which, if left alone, tend to grow in a conical shape with a point or spire at the top.

As would be expected native trees and shrubs figure prominently in field names. The many including these need no explanation: alder, ash, oak, gorse, hawthorn, hazel, sycamore and elder. In Kirk Ireton there is a field called Deaf Hazel

Meadow, referring not to a person with a hearing disability, but refers to a hazel that produces nuts without kernels.

It is, perhaps, surprising to find Apple Orchard in Matlock, Cherry Orchard in Fenny Bentley, and a plain Orchard in Chapel-en-le-Frith and Flash, as this is a type of horticulture or arboriculture generally associated with the more southerly counties. There is also a Pippen in Eyam, which could well be an apple tree raised from seed known as a pippin.

Other fruit trees named are Crabtree Piece in Hathersage which is the sour little crab-apple so beloved of wine and jelly makers; Bullacetree in Matlock refers to the wild plum, which is not a great deal bigger than a sloe.

Where ashen is found in a name it means the ash tree, and although rowan is conspicuous by its absence, the alternative name wicken does occur. Hazlebadge, pronounced hazzle-badge, is the hazel valley. The alder was also known as the owler, and that tree prized by winemakers for its flowers and berries, the elder, gives rise to field names containing ell, eller or ellen.

Gorzy is another form of gorse(y), and fields containing a willow, which besides being known as withers and withy can be identified by names derived from the Old English words 'salh' and 'saliht' – sallad, sallow and sally. Like the alder, a willow tree gives a useful indicator that the ground is wet.

It seems unlikely that Cinnamon Hill in Brassington had suitable conditions for growing this native Sri Lankan tree, and one wonders whether the ground here is yellow-brown like cinnamon, or perhaps the domesticated fowl (something like cochins) were kept here. But here it is perhaps too easy to fall into the dangerous trap of flights of fancy and guesswork.

A field in Hope simply called Shrogs means brushwood; Barbary Gutter in Staffordshire refers to the prickly berberis plant, and Quicksets in King Sterndale means hawthorn trees. The hawthorn grows prolifically in Derbyshire, being used by the Anglo-Saxons as a boundary marker and by landowners during the Enclosure Movement. It is a really tough tree, able to grow in the harshest conditions, and just outside the Peak District, in Melbourne, train loads of quickthorn were grown and dispatched all over the British Isles to be used as hedging on the railways.

At Outseats there is a Nut Ings, which is pasture land with nut trees, but it is not clear from the name which sort of tree bore the fruit. A field with a strange tree-connected name is Toilet Wood in Matlock, and once again the fertile imagination could run wild trying to find an explanation for this one.

7
FLOWER POWER

Fennel is a yellow-flowered umbelliferous plant, the seeds and aniseed-tasting leaves of which are used for seasoning. It is thought that the Romans brought this plant with them to Britain, and it was used in herbal medicine to bathe sore eyes and to aid digestion and dispel flatulence. It can be found in a street name in Ashford-in-the-Water.

The fibres of the annual flax, or *linum* to give it its Latin name, have long been used to weave into linen cloth. Originating in Egypt, it arrived in England about 1BC, and Henry VIII ordered it to be grown by statute in 1533. There was a revival in the cultivation of flax during the American Civil War, when there was a dearth of cotton, and it now seems to be enjoying a revival in some parts of the country as farmers seek alternative crops. It also can yield linseed oil, so familiar to cricketers for oiling their bats, and linoleum derives its title from this raw material which is used in its manufacture.

Lin Dale was one of the places where it could previously be found, but oddly enough not in Linen Dale, which is probably the 'lime-tree valley'. Linacre was another area of cultivated flax growing. The name Flake Pits in Rainow also indicates the processing of flax – they were pits with a fire which heated hurdles placed over them on which to dry the flax.

Parsley Hay on the High Peak Trail, the enclosure where the parsley grows, could refer to garden parsley or it could allude to the abundant growth of cow parsley which is so familiar in this part of the world. On reflection, it would seem to refer to the herb which we grow in our kitchen gardens, otherwise it would be too common to define a particular place. Another garden vegetable can be found in both Pease Close in Castleton and Peaseland Rocks in Dovedale.

The way of identifying places by the flora and fauna to be found growing there is a quite obvious one, after which an additional description of the landscape at that place will further pinpoint it, like Pease Bongs (the peas banks) in Hope.

Before electricity and gas supplies were commonplace, lighting was by means of candles and rush lights. Candlerush Edge was clearly a place where the common rush, otherwise known as candlerush that was used for rush lights, was found. Bent is also a small reed-like grass that gives its name to Fenny Bentley, 'marshy clearing with reeds', and Benty Grange, 'grange where the bent-grass grows'; more generally, 'bent' can mean any grassy pasture land.

Rough grassland is signified by the name Rowlee, and Rod Moor is simply 'reed moor'. Reeds are also mentioned in Rusden, 'rushy valley'; Rushop, 'valley where rushes grow'; and Rushton Spencer 'settlement by the rushes', with the later addition of the name of the Lords of the Manor, the Despencers. Thatch Meadows in Pilsley refers to material for thatching, which obviously would be a reed-like crop.

In the Staffordshire Moorlands, one hears people refer to coarse tussocky grass and reeds as sniddles, and looking around the place with this name it does indeed seem to be just what that means – land with coarse grass. Another indication of tussocky grass is place-names containing 'hob', even though Hob does have other explanations which we will investigate later.

Heath is land clothed with shrubby plants, especially heather and the related plants, heath, and ling. Heather has had a variety of uses, including making intoxicating drinks, animal fodder, heating fuel, thatching material, packing (of, for example, millstones), and it is a wonderful habitat for honey bees. Heathy Lee; Heathcote, 'heath cottage', and Haddon, 'heath hill' all relate to heath. Contrary to popular belief Hathersage does not mean 'heather's edge' despite it probably being an apt description, but is the 'ridge of the he-goat'.

Behind the Royal Cottage on the moors between Buxton and Leek is a field called Bareleg Hill, and it is probably so-named because in this area old heather stalks are called bare-legs and are gathered for tinder, although the usual explanation is given elsewhere in this book.

Flag Dale comes from the plant, flag being an alternative name for the iris. Irises grow in wet meadows, and this gives an idea of the terrain as well, in earlier times flag was used to describe any reed or rush. However, the village of Flagg is thought to mean 'place where the turfs were cut'; they would have been cut out in slabs, and we still use a variation of the word for stone slabs, or flags. It is quite apparent how Nettlebeds came to be named.

Parsley was to be found at Parsley Hay, while cress could be gathered from the Cressbrook and possibly Carsington, which is thought to mean 'cress farm'.

Other foods were to be found at Cranberry Clough; Barmoor Clough, 'berry moor'; Wimberry, an alternative name for bilberry, an important harvest years ago, and Cowberry Tor, which uses another name for the bilberry. Cloudberry (Moor) is a rather tasteless orange-coloured fruit that takes its name from the Old English 'cloud' meaning a hill.

The old name for wild garlic was 'hransom', and this is the first element in Ramsden. Ram is the Norse word for pungent. The plant which always elicits comments when encountered, because of its strong aniseed smell, is fennel; this was introduced by the Romans and gives us the name 'Finkle'.

Both Rue Hayes and Rudyard were called after the herb rue, which had many medicinal uses and was also used as a disinfectant. Fernilee is exactly as it sounds, 'ferny clearing', and Goldsitch is the 'golden stream'. The accepted explanation is that the gold refers to a profusion of marigolds – presumably the weed, corn marigold – which must have bloomed in profusion along the banks of the Black Brook. Even so, as pointed out to the author, when viewing Goldsitch Moss from the Roaches with a low, winter sun shining on the grass, the whole area glows golden. Goatscliff near Stoke was known as Goldcliff in 1573, and is also believed to be a marigold bank. Similarly, the field in the Buxton area called Yellow Piece might well have been a riot of buttercups.

Whin is sometimes found in field names and is another name for gorse, which would also provide a cloth of gold over the landscape. The name lives on in the whinchat bird which favours gorse as a habitat.

FIELDS

It needs no imagination to see that some fields are named after plants or vegetation that grew there. To list a few of the obvious ones, we have Lavender Knob, Bilberry Bank, Cranberry Intake, Ferny Hay, Brackeny Close, Thistly Close, Sorrel, Foxgloves, Yarrow Close, and Aniseed. Dill Acres could be the herb now found in supermarkets or it could have been any similar vetch, which were often grown to cut as green feed for horses.

It comes as a surprise to find a Dock Yard in the middle of England at Wormhill; this clearly refers to the dock that everyone uses to soothe nettle stings. The Patient Dock Croft to be found in Chapel-en-le-Frith is a different variety of dock which was used as a pot herb. Batterdock, on the other hand, is another name for what is commonly called elephants' ears

35

or wild rhubarb, in other words butterbur. Before refrigeration became widespread it was common practice to wrap butter in the leaves of this plant to keep it cool.

Other fields are named Nettles, and they were used as a green dye, and when young to make nettle soup to 'cleanse the blood'. Woad was cultivated for the blue dye that could be made from it, despite its yellow, rape-like flowers. Wad Croft in Wessington tells us that this was the field where it was grown.

8

FUR AND FEATHER

Where there are plants there are birds, and it would be an interesting exercise to see how many of a particular species still inhabit the sites named after them. Not much chance of seeing eagles at Yarncliff near Grindleford today, one suspects, but yarn is the old term for that bird, as is hern, Hernstone being 'eagle stone'. The odds of seeing crows at Crakelow in Tissington, Cracknowle in Hassop, or Cracken Edge near Chinley, would be considerably better.

And is there a rookery in the small wood at Crawshaw? Some people, like the author's grandfather, still call the thrush a throstle, which makes the meaning of Throstle Bank in Hayfield patently clear.

Continuing the feathered theme we have Lapwing Farm, Pheasants' Clough, Hawk's Nest and Hawkslee. Less obviously, Yarncliff near Grindleford and Yarnshaw both contain the dialect word 'yarn', meaning an eagle. Conkesbury (earlier Crancesbury) and Cronkston (probably Crane's Hill) are believed to be named from the crane, a heron-like bird that was commonly found in England until the 1600s.

Crowden, Crawshaw, Crakelow, and Cracken Edge are respectively 'crow valley', 'crow wood', 'crow hill', and 'crow edge'. Although Crowstones might mean 'stones where the crows gather', crowstone is another name for ganister, a hard, white, flinty stone previously used for road making and for furnace hearths.

It is sometimes guessed that Buntingfield near Ashover refers to the field bunting, whereas it is from the Bunting family name common in that district. Pye is a variant of magpie, and is found in Pyegreave, Chapel-en-le-Frith, which must have been 'abounding' with magpies to have been called that. The Pott family added their name to Shrigley (Pott Shrigley) which is 'shrike field' – the actual original Old English word is scric, which could be equally be interpreted as a mistle thrush or a corncrake.

Another name for the blackbird is ouzel, which is found in Ouzleden (blackbird valley) in the Hope Woodlands, ravens were once plentiful in Rainow (raven ridge), and the delicious sounding Custard Field might refer to a large apple (costard) or more probably the wood pigeon (cuscote). The Minstrel of the Peak, William Newton, was born at Cockey Farm, Abney, which was a 'cockbird enclosure', but Hen Cloud near the Roaches has no connection with poultry, merely meaning 'high, or steep, hill'.

Even the humble sparrow warrants a mention. The previous name of Spar Bent was Sparrow Bent, meaning long grass with many sparrows. Isn't it plain that Endcliffe Wood in Bakewell is at the end of a cliff? Well, no. The Old English for a duck is 'ened', and the earlier name was Enedeclif meaning the sloping ground where ducks are to be found. Endmoor in Monyash likewise was Henmore in 1776, being the moor of the water-hen. And Swan Rake near Hollinsclough has no connection with swans other than the fact that it is shaped like a swan's neck.

Our creature friends contribute a fair number of place-names, ranging from the birds of the air to creepy-crawlies, as in Adders Green. The smallest creature is probably the frog closely followed by the mouse. Froggatt is thought to be 'frog cottage', Froghall is 'the hollow of the frogs' while Musden is 'valley of the mice'.

There were no doubt fewer mice at Cats Tor, Catcliff and Cat Hole. The last wild cats at Cathole in Holymoorside are though to have been killed in 1860. Quite near Cat Hole is Dog Hole and it is interesting to note that Holymoor Road, in Holymoorside, was until the 1930s called Dog Hole Lane, which apparently isn't really the sort of name you would choose as your address.

A previous name of Two Dales was Toadholes, which doesn't allude to amphibians but to the fox, 'fox earth'. This was apparently changed by the Revd Daniel Vawdry. Toad in place-names often means 'fox', and comes from 'tod' the old country name for a fox which is still found in some northern dialects. Fox House, despite the pub sign showing a fox in a kennel or house, has no connection with this animal; it derives its name from George Fox who had a shepherd's hut here in 1733.

The origin of nearby Toad's Mouth is plain to see when one is there. The large roadside boulder overlooking the road is toad shaped and man has enhanced its appearance by carving an eye to complete this otherwise natural sculpture.

The small village of Foxt was at one time the 'foxes' lair'. The fox population must have been delighted at the additional source of food when the Normans brought rabbits to these islands in the twelfth century. The rabbit was then known as the coney, which rhymed with bunny, and it was not until the nineteenth century that the pronunciation changed so that it rhymed with phoney. In the past the young conies were called rabbits; it was only later that it became the accepted name for all ages of coney.

Evidence of rabbit population is found in Cunnery, Warren, and Cunning Dale, although it has been postulated that the last named could mean King's (Konig) Dale. A cunnery is the same as a warren, that is an area of ground kept for breeding rabbits, a valuable source of food and fur in the Middle Ages and protected by strict game laws.

The rabbit's larger and faster relative, the hare, is also remembered in Harrop (hare valley), Harwood (hare wood), Harecops, and Harden. Soles Hollow must have had some attraction for animals as it means 'animals' wallowing place', coming from the Old English word sol, meaning miry.

Other earth-bound creatures include the hedgehog, which used to be known by a name now reserved for scruffy little brats – urchin, and there is an Urchin Clough in the Hope Woodlands and in Charlesworth.

Darley means 'clearing frequented by animals', while Ramshaw is said to mean 'wood where the tup lives', although feasibly it could mean 'garlic wood'. There is little doubt that Bagshaw is 'badger copse', and that Beresford is 'beaver's ford'. Wolf Edge and Wolf's Pit speak for themselves; less obvious is the meaning of Woolley – 'wolves' clearing'.

Not surprisingly for a landlocked area such as the Peak, the 'seal' in Seal Edge on Kinder Scout has no connection with aquatic mammals; in this case it has the alternative meaning of 'willows'. Buxton was recorded as Buckestones in the twelfth century and, although some say it means 'rocking stone', is generally accepted to mean buck (male deer) stone. Of course, the county town of Derby denotes a deer farm. Evidence of the catching of deer remains in the name Buxter Stoops Farm. It is a corruption of a deer trap called a 'buck-stall', that is to say a net for trapping deer as they ran, which was suspended between two posts or stoops.

9
REMAINS OF INDUSTRY

Two of the principal traditional extractive industries of the Peak District were lead mining and quarrying, and they have left names in many parts of the area.

Stonegravels in Chesterfield was obviously a stone quarry, and Roach Farm near Uppertown, Ashover, was known as Peyustonhurstroche in 1543, i.e. Peasunhurst Rocks, and doubtless referred to the two quarries sited here.

Excavation for other natural materials was carried out at Gravel Pit Close in Kirk Ireton, and the fields throughout the area called Slate Pit. At Grindlestone Close in Brampton suitable rock for grindstones was found. There probably isn't any flint in the Wirksworth area although in earlier times any hard stone was called flint, but there is a Flint Close, and as Flint was a local surname it was possibly the owner's name. Bakestone Clough was the place where bakestones were quarried. Oatcakes were traditionally cooked on a back-stun or bakestone which could be thin and round to hang over the cottage fire on a trivet, or for more spacious kitchens they could be large oblong slabs to sit on top of the stove. According to John Farey Sen. in 1811, the smaller ones from Bakestone Clough were 15–16 inches in diameter, a quarter of an inch thick and sold for a shilling (5p), and the larger ones were 3 inches long by 22 inches broad and sold for 5s.6d. (27$\frac{1}{2}$p). Of course this wasn't the only quarry to produce bakestones; some others were at Birchover, Ashover, Rowlee and Beeley.

Chert is a flint-like stone which was useful to the pottery industry in Stoke on Trent, and reference to this can be found in Chertpit Plantation and Chert Pit Lane near Little Longstone. Another mineral, calamine, was mined in places such as Chrome Hill and taken to be ground at the 'cally mill' in Milldale. In British mining terms, calamine is zinc carbonate, as witnessed by Calamine Piece in Brassington and possibly in Cromford where a Calamini Close is to be found. Anyone of the author's generation will be familiar with a pinkish-white liquid preparation known as calamine lotion, which was rubbed on the skin to counteract sunburn, chickenpox spots and other dermatological conditions.

Millers Dale had two water-mills which were used for grinding corn, the one for Tideswell folk being opposite the Angler's Rest, and the one for the people of

Wormhill being at the other end of the village. It is now a centre for craft supplies.

The town of New Mills developed from the name of the Berde corn mill, or New Mill, first recorded in 1391. When other mills were opened along the River Sett 'mill' became pluralised so that in the eighteenth century the name New Mills was being used. The pub name Little Mill in Rowarth and the adjacent replica 36ft (11m) waterwheel, testify to the former cotton mill industry in this quiet backwater, where surprisingly there were once six mills. Grangemill was the mill belonging to Ivonbrook Grange.

Water-mills seem to be the preferred way of grinding corn in the Peak, with precious few windmills. The hamlet of Windmill must have had a windmill, and what a perfect site, as Wyndmilne Howse was recorded as existing in 1607.

Names such as Millstone Edge serve to remind us that quarrying and shaping millstones was a major industry in the Peak, only dying out when finer French millstones were imported in the eighteenth century. Nothing changes, eh? Having said that, there was still some minor millstone production until the early twentieth century.

At first sight Cacklemackle in Great Longstone would suggest the keeping of fowls, but in fact it is a miners' name for the worst type of lead ore, which was to be found in this field. There was a small settlement of lead miners somewhere near the Miners' Standard in Winster which went under the name Islington. In fact the Portway from here to Elton is still called Islington Lane; it is probable that the name was transferred by the miners from their home city, as they were employed by the London Lead Company.

Lead mining was a major activity in the White Peak, but a survey of field names shows that it was not the sole industry. Another useful clue to the presence of a lead mine is the name sough, as at Calver Sough (pronounced suff), which indicates a drainage outlet from a mine.

An essential requirement of mining, and generally useful elsewhere, was rope. Rope and Rope Walk are found throughout the White Peak, a rope walk being a stretch of ground along which the rope makers walked back and forth gradually releasing fibres carried around their waist onto a contraption which made strands, which were then woven into rope. A demonstration of this technique can often be seen inside the entrance to Peak Cavern in Castleton.

41

As we all know lead is a toxic material, hence the replacement of leaded petrol, and the old miners and farmers were well aware of this but couldn't do a thing about it if they didn't want to starve. Belland or belond is a local name for lead poisoning. In other parts of the country, and occasionally here, a rake is a path up a hillside but in the limestone area of the Peak District it signifies a vein of lead ore running across country which has been excavated. Lead ore, or galena, is found in vertical veins and it was dug out along the straight line of the deposit. The grooves and mounds still being plain to see, usually running in an east–west direction.

A lead mining excavation, known as a rake, near Little Hucklow

Bole Field in Kirk Ireton testifies to lead smelting being carried out; there is also a Smelting Mill Piece in Wirksworth. Bole Hill is to be found in a number of places – at least ten. A bole was a primitive wind-hearth usually sited at about 900 feet above the sea to face a constant south-westerly wind, or draught. Pudding Pie Hill gained its name from a type of bole, the remains of which are still to be found. Pudding-pie can also mean 'soft, sticky ground', but not in this case.

A successor to the bole was the cupola furnace and this name can be found in fields in Eyam, Ashover and Bradwell. Wherever the word 'cinder' occurs it is usually suffixed by 'hills', and this does lead one to surmise that the cinder or slag from furnaces has been heaped up on this land.

There is a place-name, and a fine brew of beer, called Whim, and it is unclear whether this relates to the horse-powered winding wheel, or to the horse gin used at lead mines or, as is often the case, to gorse bushes variously called whin or whim. The magnificent, sylvan Dimmingsdale, with its tranquil pools, was once a centre of copper smelting, and nearby is Old Furnace one of the first industrial sites in the Staffordshire Moorlands, dating from 1593. The firm of Thomas Boulton & Sons, who made the first trans-Atlantic underwater communications cable, still operates in the area at Oakamoor in Staffordshire.

Tanning of hides would have been done locally throughout the Peak, as is evidenced by the name Tanyard. Wheston is thought to be from whetstone, a stone for sharpening knives and scythes.

There is a wide range of fields containing either the word kill or kiln, which could, of course, be used for many purposes, but it is a pretty safe bet to say that they were employed in lime burning. In addition to these there are very many fields which are more specifically named Lime or Limekiln. Wirksworth and Bakewell both have a Brick Kiln Close, harking back to the days when bricks were made locally.

Before the railway age gave access to the major coal-mining areas of Britain, coal had to be dug locally; it was usually of poor quality but served its purpose. In Foolow, Wirksworth, Alderwasley and Pott Shrigley 'coal pit' is incorporated into field names. At Chapel-en-le-Frith, Colshaw could refer to coal digging or to charcoal burning.

Industry involving cloth is recalled by Walkmile Croft in Ashford-in-the-Water and Walkmill in Wirksworth. A walkmile was a fulling mill, so named because workers walked up and down to tread into the cloth a hydrous silicate of alumina known as fuller's earth (now used as cat litter), which cleansed and thickened the cloth. Incidentally, the previous process to the fulling was to soak the wool in urine to remove the natural oil. Later fulling mills replaced walkers with wooden drop hammers which pounded the fuller's earth into the cloth.

Cloth was stretched by means of hooks on a frame of upright poles known as a tenter, from the Latin *tendere* to stretch, to keep its shape while drying. We are all familiar with the saying 'on tenterhooks', for someone who is left in suspense. A tenter was a wooden framework for stretching cloth by means of hooks or bent nails so that it would dry evenly without shrinking. This process took place at Tenterhill and is also the origin of Trentabank, near Macclesfield, recorded in 1831 as Tenter Bank. In Tainter Piece in Chinley and the many other Tenter or Tentry yards, fields or crofts mark the sites of this work.

In Matlock there is both a Calender Close (a calendar is a machine for smoothing woollen cloth to give it a gloss) and a Bleach Yard. A Bump Mill field is to be found in Ashover and another in Bradwell; bump is a material made of strands of cotton, or refuse flax, loosely twisted together. One of the uses was for candlewick and bump-sheets, which had thick fibres going one way and much thinner fibres crossing the other way, which meant that if they weren't wrung out in the right direction they tore easily.

Other signs of industrial activity in field names include a Dam Close in Eyam; a Dyehouse Meadow in Kettleshulme; a Factory Close in Crich; two Engine Closes, one in Wensley and the other in Great Longstone, which no doubt refer to engine houses for lead mines. There is also an Engine Field in Bollington, as well as one in Edale. Perhaps the latter had some connection with the steam engine that was transported by road over Mam Nick to Edale when the railway was being constructed. There is a Rollingmill Field in Matlock. Old Engine Farm at Ashover was the site for the pump for the Gregory Mine. There is a Sowter Butts in Monyash, a sowter being a shoemaker, though he probably plied his trade elsewhere but owned the field.

Elsewhere on maps we find reference to a Slitting Mill and Iron Pits. Cowley is the col or coal lea, the clearing where charcoal was burnt. There is a name Coal Hills in Wirksworth, and this too would relate to charcoal burning as there is no black coal there.

There is even a Wheal: this must be a name for a mine transferred from the West Country by Cornish miners. A considerable exchange of labour went on between Devon and Cornwall and Derbyshire, and one has only to look at the architecture of Magpie Mine, near Sheldon, or listen to the tune played at Castleton Garland Ceremony to see the connection. It is almost identical to that of the Cornish Floral Dance.

10

DOWN ON THE FARM

Many place-names give us an insight into the agricultural uses of land in days of yore, as well as the farmers' opinion of the state of their land, and even the rent they paid.

First of all, there is the Old English word tun, or ton, which is variously taken to mean village, estate, or farm though presumably the farm would usually have been the first dwelling, making that the most accurate interpretation. So we have, for example, Shatton (farmstead in a corner of land); Gratton (big, great, farm); Litton (farm on a slope or hillside); Aston (east farm); Coldeaton (cold farm by a stream); Walton (farm of the Welshman), and Bretton (farm of the Britons). It has also been suggested that Bretton might be named after Roger Breton, a knight of the Peverels.

Evidence of cattle husbandry is found in the names Calver (pronounced 'Carver') meaning 'calf slop', and Cauldon Low meaning 'calf hill'. Kid Lands in Kirk Ireton does not have any connection with goats, but was where the sucking calves were kept. Both Hargate at Wormhill and Charlesworth, and Hardwick mean 'herd farm' and Hargatewall is the 'spring by the herd farm'.

The suffix 'wick' denotes a dairy farm; Knightwake in New Mills comes from Knight Wick, being the dairy farm of the young men. Milking Lane and Milken Lane show the way the milkers took.

Other bovine place- and field names include Ox Pasture at Hassop and Great Hucklow; Oxlow in Peak Forest; Ox Hey in Bosley; Bullock Close in Matlock; Cow Close at Offerton; Calf Croft in Hartington Middle Quarter; Steer Close in Matlock, and a Steer Croft in Monyash; Bullshaw and Bull Stake. Oxgang appears in Shottle, but this is a land measure, being one-eighth of a carucate (a carucate was the amount of land ploughed by a team of eight oxen, so an eighth was deemed to be the amount ploughed by one ox). Birley (Farm) at Outseats means the byre clearing, a byre being a shippon or cow-house. Then there is Butterton; Butterlands in Wincle; Butterley; Smerrill (good pasturage hill); Greenlands in Chinley and Edale; Green Cowden (cow hill) near Bakewell; Eatage Close (good grazing land) in

Tansley; Summerhill (summer grazing), and Meadow Place in Youlgreave, all of which give a picture of where the beasts were kept.

Horsley is simply the horse pasture, and sheep farming is confirmed by such names as Lamber Close in Ible and Lamberlands (lambs) at Mapleton; Ewe Lee in the Eyam Woodlands; Ship Loads (sheep stream) in Matlock; Shepton Croft (sheep enclosure), and Tup Paddock in Tissington.

An interesting name is Lockers Clough, meaning shepherd's dell: a locker or looker was a person who looked after flocks of sheep, and as far as I know this is the only example of this word being used in the Peak District, as it is usually found in the southern counties of England.

Oyster Clough in the Hope Woodlands owes its name to an Old English word for a sheep 'eowestre', and would be where the sheepfold or pen was located. Bolt Edge at Chapel has a similar meaning, bolt being a dialect term for a sheepfold. Sheep were marked with red dye known as ruddle, and the place it was dug is shown in names like Ruddle Clough and Riddle Pits.

Other animals kept for food include pigs, with field names like Hoghouse Field, and Swindells (swine hills), and places like Swainsley in the Manifold Valley, Swint Clough (both referring to swine) in the Hope Woodlands, Hogshaw in Fairfield and Pictor in Green Fairfield, which was formerly Pig Tor. Lose Hill is thought to derive from the Old English word for a pigsty, 'hlose', the same applies to Lousy Field in Chapel-en-le-Frith.

Some maps show the name 'Pinfold'. A pinfold, or pound, was a small stone-walled pen or fold where stray animals were kept until claimed by their rightful owner on payment of a fine to the keeper of the pinfold, who was called the pinder. If the fine wasn't paid the animal could be either kept or sold. They were usually sited on the edge of a village; preserved examples are at Biggin, Birchover, Castleton, Chelmorton, Curbar, Eyam, Hathersage, Hope, Thorpe, and Youlgreave. Pinder's Rock near Brassington has no connection with this custom; in the eighteenth century it belonged to a woman called Jane Pindar.

References to goats are sparse, but Hathersage is 'he-goats' ridge', and there is a Goats Nook. Evidence of keeping birds is provided by Fowls Croft in Over Haddon, Chicken Meadow in Tissington , Goose Meadow in Bradbourne, Goose Close in both Eyam and Crich, and Capon Roods in Sheldon. For those brought up in the supermarket age when all poultry is called 'chicken', it should be explained that a capon is a castrated cock fattened for eating.

As regards arable farming, no doubt the crops grown on a particular field varied over the years, but at least at one stage of its history it was suitable for the one named. It is a fascinating thought that the Celts grew peas, beans and grain, but it was not until they were introduced to these islands by the Romans that such everyday vegetables and fruit as cabbage, carrot, celery, parsnips, turnips, apples and pears were grown.

The humble swede does not seem to be mentioned in any field name, although it could be covered by the general term 'turnip', as its proper name is the Swedish turnip. There are a goodly number of Turnip Fields, even more Cornfields, Corn Closes, and a Wheat Piece at Ashover. Other grains include many Rye Tang, Closes, or Crofts, including a field in Little Longstone called Rioth which in 1611 was known as Rie Earth. Rye was also grown at Riber, 'rye hill', and Riley 'rye land', near Eyam. Riley is where the Riley Graves are situated, and is the obvious reason they are so-called despite the interred plague victims all being from a family named Hancock.

Hayfield was clearly the place where the hay was harvested. The places called Pilhough show that pill oats were cultivated, as does Pillow Butts in Wirksworth, and there are a couple of instances of Oat Close, in Matlock and Alderwasley. Matlock has a Cabbage Close, and Cromford has a Beet, and Potato Fields are found throughout the Peak. One of the most plentiful mentions is Barley with six fields found before the author stopped counting, and a Barley Hill.

Beans too were grown at Bean Beatings in Hope – but bean meaning turf is found in Bean Clough in Bosley, Bean Hill at Castleton, Bean Lands in Eyam, and Bean Row. Barlow is the 'barley clearing', although once again there is another interpretation of 'boar clearing'. Banafurlong in Great Longstone also derives from the Old English word for a bean.

Of the numerous Peas or Pease found, the delightful-sounding Peas Bongs was not uncommon suggesting that peas were often grown on banks. Peaseland (Rocks) in Dovedale is the marsh where the peas grew, while Peasunhurst, despite peason being a dialect word for peas, is apparently not connected with the legumes; it is said to be 'Paega's stone and wood'. Peasebread was a staple of the peasant class, whereas the better off would have 'proper' bread.

There is a Lentil Close in Alderwasley and a Lentil Hill in Wessington. It would be easy to conclude that the climate has worsened dramatically on finding Lemon Cliff in Kirk Ireton, but sadly this does not refer to a fruit but to an artificial watercourse, a lemon or leme. We do not know whether Strawberry in Wessington and Strawberry Lee in Great Longstone grew the fruit as a crop or it was where they grew naturally.

Colourful fields would have been seen at Mustard Close in Tideswell, the various Clover Fields, Rape in Ashover, and the numerous Flax Fields. Hemp Yard is quite common, yard being a field rather than a slabbed area. Hemp, or *Cannabis sativa* to give it its full title, is a narcotic drug which was commonly used in herbalism and by orthodox medicine, until the first half of the twentieth century, as a tranquilliser. However, in this area it would have been grown for its fibrous quality, which made it ideal for spinning into ropes to be used mainly in the lead mining industry.

Hops were introduced to England in the late Middle Ages, and were far more extensively grown around the 1500s for their herbal properties as a sedative or soporific, as anyone who has ever used a hop-pillow will testify, and to give a bitter flavour to beer. Before tea and coffee became popular, beer was a regular drink throughout the day, even having a weak brew called 'small beer' at breakfast time. There are fields called Hopyard in Kniveton and Ashover. A yard was a measurement of land equivalent to about a quarter of an acre, enough to grow 500 hop plants.

Plex Farm near Buxton was called Hopping Pleckes in 1614, which denotes a small field where hops grew, and there is a Hopping Farm near Youlgreave. Whether Brosterfield Farm, Housley, grew hops is not clear, but the land belonged to a brewer, having the former name of Brewsterfeld.

Naturally, crops need fertilizer for successful growth, and this too is mentioned in names. The Dunge Brook flows through well-manured land, and Shooterslea, Ashover, was previously named Shitersley with a similar meaning. The field name Midding Croft in Wildboarclough relates to midden, or muck to use the vernacular. Midding not only included animal and human waste, but things such as broken pottery, so when it was spread on the fields the pottery, for example, can still be found leading to false assumptions about 'lost villages'. Mixon, Dunge at Thornhill, Dingers Hollow, from dyngja meaning dung, and Shittern Clough near Glossop, all have related meanings.

Land which was unproductive had a variety of uncomplimentary names, one of the most common being 'hungry', meaning that it was poor land which needed manuring to make it worthwhile for cultivation. The farmer who named Mount Famine presumably had a lean time of it too.

One way of increasing the productivity and fertility of land is to clear it by burning, and planting in the resultant ashes, a process was called 'slash and burn'. Brand and Brund both mean burned, and Brunswood at Kniveton, is 'burnt wood'. Brandy Lee Farm gets its name because at some stage in its history a meadow was created by burning woodland. Swythamley is also land cleared by burning, coming from the word svitha meaning just that. Bunster also means the hill cleared of scrub by burning.

When land had been cleared it needed to be ploughed and where 'breach' is found it means that it has been ploughed to break the soil. New, as in Newlands, Little Hucklow, and New Close, also signifies once newly broken land. Highlightley was the 'high, bright clearing', and Fairfield was also 'fair open land', whilst Fallinge was land lying fallow.

Dewsnaps, near Tintwistle, is a wonderful field name which means 'dewy, wet pasture land', whilst Gall, as in Gall Pingle, Taddington, is also marshy land which is not much use agriculturally. The field in Little Longstone called Clemley Park tells us that it is wet, infertile, clay-ey soil.

The name Holme means a raised section of ground, an island if you will, in a water meadow or wet ground. Tunstead means a farmstead, and Thorpe is a Scandinavian word for an outlying farm or hamlet, while Outseats are outlying houses and probably summer pasture. The way to the outlying lands and higher ground were known as Outrakes.

A booth was a temporary herdsman's shelter, or sometimes an animal pasture in a clearing, the one belonging to the Barber family being remembered in the place name Barber Booth. There are a number of other Booth names in the Edale area.

In farming terms, the place-name 'fog' is deceptive. Grass known as Yorkshire fog has very little grazing value when young and has to be allowed to grow. This is the meaning of Fog Field in Edale – it is long grass left standing in winter.

The practice of terracing hillsides to make them suitable for crop growing is shown on maps as 'lynchets'; another word found in place-names is bench, and a holding with small ribboned fields would be called a ladder. Longrose Farm, Kniveton, when said out loud becomes obvious, it was a place with 'long rows'.

When fields' names include coinage in the their title it could indicate the rent payable at one time. Farthing Meadow in Hope might just be a small field like the coin, but there is also Penny Prick in Eyam; Penny Bank in Chapel-en-le-Frith; Penny Hill in Hathersage; and Halfpenny Croft in King Sterndale.

11
CHAPEL AND CHURCH

Not surprisingly, the Church has left clues to its history in the landscape of the Peak, whether in field, street, farm, or village names.

In 1225, foresters founded a chapel which was called the 'Chapell in the Firthe', or the chapel in the forest clearing, which became Chapel-en-le-Frith. As far as I can recall, this is the only town named after a church – the chapel in the Royal Forest of the Peak.

The author recalls on moving to Buxton, being amazed how God-fearing many of the residents were, even on Saturday saying, 'I'm going to chapel this afternoon'. It took a few weeks for the penny to drop and the realisation that they were going shopping in the neighbouring town.

Perhaps the most commonly known place-name signifying a religious connection is glebe. Unusually, this comes from a Latin word *glaeba* which simply means 'soil'. The produce of glebe land was used for the maintenance of the parish priest. It signifies land assigned to a clergyman as part of his income, or benefice. This supplemented his main source of income which was from the three types of tithes which theoretically gave him one-tenth of the income from the annual produce of land in his parish.

The involvement of the Church authorities is recorded in such names as Quakers Field in Wessington, Rood Stone in Curbar (rood in this case being another word for a cross, as in rood-screen in churches), Kirk, and Glebe Land. There is also a Vicar's Meadow in Mapleton; a Parson's Piece in Ible (although conceivably this could be a surname); Abbeylands in Chelmorton; Abbot's Park in Wessington, and a field called Priest in Great Hucklow.

The name gospel occurs in a number of places including Gospel Hillock in King Sterndale; Gospel Stone in Hathersage; Gospel Greave in Ashford and in Wheston, and Gospel Tree in Ashover. These indicate the place where the gospels were read to the assembled crowd when verifying the parish boundary.

Crosses abound in the Peak District, for whatever reason they were erected, be

Detail of the roadside cross at Wheston

it to mark territory, a market-place, a place of worship, or to guide travellers, they are essentially a Christian symbol. Lady Cross on the East Moor was probably put up by the Canons of Beauchief Abbey as it marks the boundary of their lands, and their abbey was dedicated to St Mary. There are two excellent ornate crosses at Foolow and at Wheston, the latter has a carving of the Holy Mother and Child on the reverse. Another plain but striking cross stands in Shillitoe Wood on the Eastern Moors.

Peter's Stone in Cressbrook Dale, supposedly similar to St Peter's Basilica in Rome

Good examples of older crosses stand in Bakewell, Eyam, Leek, Bradbourne, and Hope churchyards. Cleulow (Cross) probably means 'ball', from the Old English cliewen, possibly because it sits on a ball-shaped artificial mound.

A well-preserved crucifix is to be found in a shallow cave in the shade of a large yew tree at the foot of Cratcliffe Tor. This is shown on maps as Hermit's Cave. Contrary to popular belief, hermits did not live a life of total exclusion from the world, although people like Anchorites did. This hermit's cave, said to date from the twelfth century, overlooks the ancient Portway, the road to the market, (a sort of medieval motorway) and he probably blessed travellers for a suitable recompense.

Two records exist which may possibly be connected to this place. One speaks of a hermit selling conies (rabbits) at Haddon Hall in 1550, and, another, a century later, tells of a 'man of Cratcliffe' being paid by churchwardens at Youlgreave to catch conies.

Churchdale and Kirk Dale both have the same meaning, and presumably were either the route to the church, or part of their property, kirk meaning church, from the Old Norwegian kirkja. So Kirk Ireton is the church and farm of the Irishmen. Another dale with a church connection is Channon Dale in Youlgreave, which translates as Canon's Dale. Chander Hill in Holymoorside refers to a chorister or chanter, suggesting a chantry hereabouts. A chantry was a chapel where one or more priests would sing a daily mass for the souls of the wealthy founders, who would have provided an endowment for this purpose. The words camel and needle come to mind. Edward VI suppressed chantries in 1547.

It should be mentioned that the word chanter can equally apply to a magician, or enchanter. Wortley Court in Bradwell was land allotted to Wortley Chapel in 1819. On a vaguely religious note, it is claimed that Peter's Stone in Cressbrook Dale is so-called because of its physical resemblance to St Peter's Basilica in Rome. The place-name Eccles sometimes derives from to the personal name Eccel, but generally was the word used by pagan Anglo-Saxons to refer to the Christian Church. Hence 'ecclesiastic', pertaining to the Church. Eccles Pike is therefore 'church hill', although church in this instance means the gathering or congregation rather than a building. It did once have a cross on top which is now in Chapel-en-le-Frith churchyard. Eagle Tor near Stanton in Peak was once known as Eccles Tor.

Hades, Holymoorside, Hallowes, and Jericho are four names ostensibly associated with the Church, yet have no connection whatever. Hades, pronounced to rhyme with shades, is the unploughed headland in a field where the plough turned round. The hade had to be ploughed in another direction after the rest of the field had been tilled. Often the hades were left as access ways to the fields and when a number of them were joined together they would form a green lane. There is a Hades Lane in Taddington although for some reason the 'H' is painted out, and this was also the one-time name of Queens Road in Buxton.

Holymoorside is a hillside clearing if one traces the name back far enough, and Jericho is one of those names often given to places on the outskirts of the village. Hallows comes from the Old English halh, meaning a water-meadow.

Lud Church is a deep chasm or cleft in the gritstone rocks north of the Roaches. It was said to be used by the followers of John Wycliffe, the fourteenth-century religious reformer. They were known as Lollards, which is a Dutch word for

The entrance to Lud Church on the Roaches, said to be the worshipping place of the Lollards, but is the name much older than that?

'mumblers'. They were not, as is often stated, Luddites, who were the followers of Ned Ludd, a worker who destroyed textile machines in the early nineteenth century as a protest against mechanisation.

The reason for the name Lud Church is not known for certain. It is claimed that it was named after Walter de Lud-Auk who was preaching when soldiers broke up a meeting there in 1405. According to a report written 140 years after the event by Sir William de Lacey, Walter's granddaughter, Alice, was killed in the raid, and buried at the entrance to the 'church', and he was captured and died in prison. Could it be that Walter was named after the 'church' instead of the other way round? De Lud-Auk means of the Lud Church, if, as I am told, auk is an Old English word for a church.

Another explanation is that Lud, Llud, or Lugh was a Celtic deity equivalent to Thor in Norse mythology. The supposition that the sun only shines directly into the chasm at the summer solstice would seem appropriate for a sun god. What is interesting is that the surrounding countryside fits very nicely into descriptions of places in the medieval poem, 'Sir Gawain and the Green Knight', and was almost certainly written about this area. Sir Gawain has his final encounter with the Green Knight here in the Green Church.

Houndkirk was formerly Ankirk, which is 'giant's church', but just what the church was or who the giant was is unknown.

Jenkin Chapel, dedicated to St John the Baptist, was erected in 1733 at Jenkins Cross. It is said that Jenkins was a drover and preacher who walked his sheep to the Peak District from Ruthin in Wales in the eighteenth century. He may well have done, but the place was known as 'Jankynscros' as long ago as 1364.

There was no temple at Temple Normanton. Normanton tells us that it was 'the farm of the Norwegians', and temple that it was an estate or hospice belonging to the medieval religious and military order, the Knights Templar.

Years ago it was customary to 'beat the bounds' of a parish. Boundary markers were visited, and at each mark children were helped to remember the location of these places by a variety of means. They were tipped upside down, given sweets, stung with stinging nettles, smacked and suchlike to help them remember the boundary points, and the Gospels were read by the church official. After the fields were enclosed, it would have become more difficult to follow the line of the boundary, but the many places including the name Gospel recall the place where the Bible reading was given.

Jenkin Chapel, erected in 1733 – but who was Jenkin? This place was known as Jankynscros in 1364

A field in Ashover called Elmit land is thought to mean 'hermit's marsh'. Both Nunsfield Farm and Nun Brook, relate to grazing land at Fairfield, which was granted to the nuns of King's Mead Priory, Derby in the thirteenth century.

Throughout the Peak District, various monastic brotherhoods had granges. A grange was a farm belonging to a monastery although they were frequently tenanted by lay brethren and hired hands because of their remoteness from the religious establishment which owned them. Mostly the farms were sheep farms, or becaries, and they both fed and clothed the monks, but also generated income for the owners. It was the Cistercians, or White Monks, who started this system after being given vast areas of land by the Normans. Other religious orders copied the idea.

HOME ON THE GRANGE

The following list shows the names of some of the granges, the abbey to which they belonged and the relative religious order.

RELIGIOUS ORDER	GRANGE	ABBEY
Augustinian	Aldwark Grange	Darley Abbey
	Bradbourne Grange,	Dunstable Priory, Beds.
	Conksbury Grange	Leicester Abbey
	Crich Grange	Darley Abbey
	Grindlow Grange	Lilleshall Abbey, Salop.
	Hardwick Grange	Newstead Priory, Notts.
	Meadow Place Grange	Leicester Abbey
	Middleton Grange	Leicester Abbey
	Mouldridge Grange	Dunstable Priory, Beds.
	Scarcliffe Grange	Newstead Priory, Notts.
	Smerrill Grange	Leicester Abbey
	(probably)	
	Wessington Grange	Darley Abbey
	Wigwell Grange	Darley Abbey
Benedictine	Hanson Grange	Burton Abbey, Staffs.
Cistercian	Abney Grange	Rufford Abbey, Notts.
	Barlow Grange	Louth Abbey, Lincs.
	Biggin Grange	Garendon Abbey, Leics.
	Calling Low Grange	Roche Abbey, Yorks.
	Cotesfield Grange	Combermere Abbey, Ches.
	Cronkston Grange	Merevale Abbey, Warks.
	Heathcote Grange	Garendon Abbey, Leics.
	Ivonbrook Grange	Buildwas Abbey, Salop.
	Mainstonefield Grange	Merevale Abbey, Warks.
	Mouldridge Grange	Garendon Abbey, Leics.
		(later sold to Dunstable Priory)
	Pilsbury Grange	Merevale Abbey, Warks.
	Roystone Grange	Garendon Abbey, Leics.
	Needham Grange	Merevale Abbey, Warks.
	Newton Grange	Combermere Abbey, Ches.
	One Ash Grange	Roche Abbey, Yorks.
	Pilsbury Grange	Merevale Abbey, Warks.

	Wincle Grange	Combermere Abbey, Ches
	Wolfscote Grange	Garendon Abbey, Leics
Cluniac	Monk's Dale Grange	Lenton Priory, Notts
Premonstratensian	Crookhill Grange	Welbeck Abbey, Notts
	Griffe Grange	Dale Abbey
	Harewood Grange	Beauchief Abbey, Yorks

Dieulacres Abbey, pronounced 'dew-la-cress', was a Cistercian foundation of the Earl of Chester in 1214. The name is Norman-French and is translated as 'may God give it increase'.

Smaller monasteries were suppressed in 1536, and the larger ones three years later, the chantries surviving until 1545. With this dissolution, the granges and relative land passed into the hands of the major landowners.

Just as an aside, a piece of trivia with no connection with place-names; in the 1600s a strange sect called the Muggletonians had their local headquarters at Throwley Hall in the Manifold Valley.

12
THE OLD RELIGION

There are surprisingly few places named after the old pre-Christian gods. The village of Wensley is said to be named after the same god after whom Wednesday is named, and means 'Woden's field'.

An alternative name for Woden was Grimm, and it is believed by many that the various place-names including this word relate to Woden. The goddess Frig or Frija gave her name to Friden, which was previously known as Frigdene. Frig's symbol was a boar crest, as featured on the famous Dark Age helmet found not far away at Benty Grange near Monyash, and now in the Weston Park Museum in Sheffield.

Nobody really knows when Thor's Cave in the Manifold Valley first took its name from the Norse god of thunder. But the druid Ralph de Tunstall Sneyd, who lived at Onecote, obviously thought that it had ancient connections, and reinstated the ancient Gorsedd ceremony here in the 1920s, bringing his many white-robed followers here by the Leek and Manifold Light Railway – what a sight that must have been.

Odin Mine near Castleton is the oldest recorded lead mine in Derbyshire, but that record is only in 1280. That's not far enough back to claim it was mined by the Saxons, but who would bet that they named it? The Neolithic burial chamber called the Bridestones in Staffordshire is named after the earth-goddess Bride, who was later canonised as St Brigid by the Catholic Church in an effort to eradicate the pagan goddess.

The numerous places including 'lady' in their name sometimes allude to the Virgin Mary, or Our Lady. But it is argued by many that 'Lady' is really a memory of a pagan goddess from the pre-Christian days, when people worshipped the 'Lady' or earth-mother goddess, rather than the 'Lord'.

Before John Bunting gave his name to Buntingfield in the seventeenth century, it had the more sinister name of Deueleswode, i.e. Devil's Wood. Devil's Dyke was allegedly scratched out by the Devil's claws, but in reality it is a Dark Age boundary trench. There is also a Devil's Elbow on the road from Glossop into

Longdendale, and one of the tales the locals tell of this area is of a giant slug that has been seen to cross the road here.

Still on a vaguely spiritual theme, we have a Phantoms Close in Hognaston, and a Fantom Hag in Matlock. Goblins, real or imagined, may be behind the naming of Little Men Close (elves?) in Baslow. Eldon (Hill) near Castleton derives from elf-dun, or elves' hill. Scratter above Little Longstone could come from skratti meaning a demon; even now one hears people referring to the devil as Old Scrat.

Another name for a sprite, bogey, or hobgoblin is hob, a name which constantly crops up in Peak District field names; although a more prosaic explanation is that it derives from the Old English hobbe, which is tussocky grass.

Was Hassop a place to avoid at one time? One reading of the name is that it is the 'witch valley', from the Old English haetse for a crone or woman with supernatural powers.

What is the reason for describing a place as shining, for example Shining Tor, and Shining Cliff? It is usually given as meaning 'bright and shining', but some people think that it alludes to a spectre and get quite excited when they realise that the place in Longdendale famous for mysterious lights in the hillside is called Shining Clough. Sheen is also interpreted as a 'bright, shining place'.

13
DRAWING THE BOUNDARIES

There are a number of place-names throughout the Peak District which denote a boundary. These often follow natural features and changes of landscape, and, of course, rivers, streams, and even old roads can often provide a ready-made boundary line.

The River Limb which forms part of the boundary between the episcopal jurisdictions of Canterbury and York, at one time between Northumbria and Mercia, and now Derbyshire and Yorkshire, is so-called from the Latin word *limbus,* meaning an edge or border. Limbo, the place on the edge of Hell, derives from the same root – this observation is no reflection on either county, by the way.

Mere in its various spellings can mean a pond, but it has an alternative meaning of a boundary. Two places incorporating this word are Meerbrook, which is self-explanatory, and Morledge (Farm) which gets its name from 'meare lache' or boundary stream.

Edale Cross in the snow – an ancient boundary marker and wayside cross   TERRY BETTNEY

Occasionally a dale is used as a boundary. Hall Dale marks the extent of the northern perimeter of the Hurt family's Castern Hall estate, while Marsden means 'mark valley'. Mark is another useful term for a frontier or limit, an example being Gladwin's Mark, above Beeley, which identified the bounds of land owned by William Gladwin of Ashover. Crosses appear to have a number of uses, not least that of a marker. The so-called Abbot's Chair on Monks Road, Glossop, is the base of a boundary cross erected by the monks of Basingwerk Abbey. Edale Cross was probably placed there by the same people at the southern edge of their land, and marks the divisions of the Royal Forest of the Peak, being the place where the wards of Longdendale, Hopedale and Champion meet. The initials IG and the date 1810 were incised by John Gee of Ashes Farm, when he and some fellow farmers restored the cross after finding it broken and lying on the ground. Today it is enclosed by a wall erected by its current owners, the National Trust.

Poles and trees were erected and planted to proclaim the border of an area. So we have Pole Lane, named after the Armfield pole put up by, and named after, one Robert Armfield in 1640, and Staden – 'hill marked by poles or staves' – just outside Buxton on the Ashbourne road. The prominent Stanage Pole stands on the boundary of Derbyshire and Yorkshire on the Eastern Moors.

'Tree' as part of a name frequently means that it is either a meeting place or a boundary, or even both. Tom Thorn is the parish boundary between Wormhill and Fairfield, and a map of 1770 in the Chandos-Pole-Gell collections includes the depiction of a bush here. One wonders if there is a connection with 'tom', a Gaelic word for a knoll or mound?

Horwich (End), pronounced Horridge, had a boundary marked by a wych elm, the name being derived from 'har', meaning 'grey' or 'boundary', plus wych. Use of this word 'har' is also found, but not obviously, in Warlow Pike on the Derbyshire-Yorkshire border. It was Harelowe in 1468 and means the pointed hill marking the boundary.

In Castleton, there is a Hurd Low, which has a different meaning from the other Hurdlow, near Buxton. This one also derives from the word har, meaning grey (describing the limestone?) and/or boundary. Above Beeley there is Harland (Edge) meaning boundary wood – land coming from the Old Norwegian word for a wood: 'lundr'. Rowland also includes this word 'lundr', the Row part of the name being from 'ra' the Old Norwegian for boundary, although it can mean deer too.

Yet another wood with a similar use, now lost beneath the waters of the Derwent Reservoir, was Shire Owlers Wood, which marked the boundary between the shires of

Derbyshire and Yorkshire, 'owlers' being dialect for alders. On the edge of Maccles-field Forest a farm called Eaves Farm stands on the edge or eaves of the wood.

Ball can be a boundary mound, and it is thought that Ballgreave (Farm) means 'boundary mound wood', greave in this case being a plantation of trees. Threaphurst near Marple means 'wooded hill in dispute', which would suggest a question over ownership, in other words, a boundary dispute. Similarly, there is a place lying on the boundary of Macclesfield Forest and Wildboarclough called Chest Hollow, which means disputed land in a hollow.

Some say that a cogger is a boundary wall, which would make Coggers Lane a defining line. A road which is a boundary is the one by Merryton Low on Morridge; it gradually changed names from the original Gemaere Lone, or border lane, to Meriloneslowe in the thirteenth century, to its present name. Butts Farm near Wardlow gets its name from Meane Butts, which in 1617 was a strip of land held in common and abutting a boundary.

Hearthstone is either the grey stone or the boundary stone; it is known that grey and boundary are alternative interpretations of the word 'har', and one wonders if grey does indeed signify a frontier or barrier of some kind.

Ditch, the long, narrow hollow dug out as a defensive line and boundary marker is found in various names, even simply as The Ditch as at Chelmorton, but in Bradwell both come together as Grey Ditch, which is a double ditch built sometime after the fifth century .

Natural rock features used as markers include Ilam Rock and Tissington Spires, both pinnacles of limestone in Dovedale which marked parish boundaries, and Madwoman's Stones on Kinder Scout on the Edale-Hope parish boundary. But no clues as to who she was.

Perhaps the best-known, and loved, boundary is Three Shire Heads, the picturesque spot where Staffordshire, Derbyshire and Cheshire come together in the heart of the Staffordshire moorlands. You are welcome to peruse a modern map to determine the precise place where they meet. In 1533, it is recorded that Panniers Pool was the place, by 1656 Three Shire Mears (boundary stones) was recorded, and in 1804 we are told that there were three stones on Cheeks Hill marking the meeting point.

This is a place where bare-knuckle prizefights were once held, and the contest-ants and crowds were able to nip from one county to the other if the local constabulary arrived.

Although Wainstones is invariably said to mean 'wagon stones', it is difficult to imagine wains or carts in the locations of these stones. Another suggestion is that another meaning of wain, i.e. border or hem, is more likely to indicate a boundary of some kind.

Skirt, as found near Bradley, also signifies a boundary, and the same root gives us the modern phrases of skirting board, skirting around, and outskirts.

Galleywood Bridge at Three Shires Head, the meeting point of the counties of Cheshire, Derbyshire and Staffordshire

14
FIELD NAMES

No book on place-names would be complete without a glance at the area's field names. In an age when many farmers refer to their fields by numbers or their acreage (or should that be hectarage?), it is refreshing to find that some still refer to them by old names.

Field names are a rich source for any student as a form of history not recorded elsewhere, and as a record of surnames and Christian names of long-gone people who battled the Peak District wind, snow, rain and sun to eke out a living and about whom nothing is now known.

With notable exceptions, it was not until the eighteenth century that field names were written down, because until then they were transmitted orally. It does not need much imagination to realise that fields had to be identified and described in some simple way since man began farming. Every field had a name.

The elements used in naming are many and wondrous but basically contain the following: the size of field, the tenant or owner's name, trees to be found there, prevalent vegetation, landscape features, type of soil, domesticated animals kept, industrial activity nearby, wild animals, crops grown, and occasionally the farmer's exasperated opinion of the difficulties in cultivating the plot.

What struck home on investigating the field names was the wide variety of names and the sense of humour displayed by the namers. The author must confess to not having visited, or even precisely located, the majority of these fields – that would be the work of a lifetime – but to really try to 'understand' the fields more fully it would obviously be desirable to visit them.

As has already been said, it is easy to get things wrong when dealing with any place-name, and the author is as easily misled as the next man, perhaps more so. As an example, when looking at Radish Closes in Litton, it seemed obvious that it was where the radishes were grown, but further investigation showed that it came from the Old English words ruh and edisc meaning 'rough enclosure'. It is hoped any other such hasty conclusions have been eliminated from the following.

Let's look at some instances arranged as near as possible into appropriate categories. First of all, we will look at the physical shape and size of the fields.

SHAPE AND SIZE

One of the smallest sizes would appear to be Spade Tang, in Curbar, which is 'a tongue of land a spade wide', which might be wider than Narrow Tang. Houndtail in Hartington Upper Quarter also suggests a thin strip of land, as does Strunts, Baslow, a dialect word for a tail. Slang is found in Brough and Castleton and it too signifies a narrow field.

It would be interesting to compare fields of similar meanings to see whether there is any clear distinction between the different descriptions; for example is a slipe or slip bigger or smaller than a slang?

Handkerchief is found in Cromford, Matlock and Wensley, while there is a Farthing Meadow in Hope and a Wren Park in both Ault Hucknall and Ashover, all suggesting a small area. Shoe Broad crops up in Ashford and at least two other places, and would clearly not be as big as Broad Arse Pingle in Fenny Bentley. It is plain to see from the last named, and others to follow, that the guardians of the land called a spade a spade and didn't bother to pussyfoot around with more genteel terms. Another way of describing a very small piece of land is Crimble, and among the places that this can be found is King Sterndale.

In the Edale area there are fields called Four Days Math, Four Days Work, and Five Days Math which show the size of the field by the amount of time needed to plough or mow it. Everything is relative of course, and it would be interesting to know how Mickle Flatt 'big flat land' compares to these. Turn Meadow in Bradwell, and Turna Pingle at Carsington are both circular fields, while other field shapes are described by such terms as Shoulder of Mutton in Mapleton; Elbow and Brandy Bottle, both in Great Longstone; Cockthat (cocked hat) in Bradwell, and so on. While the first part of a field name is usually descriptive of the use to which the land was put, the second element gives an idea of size.

Far from being a place of massacre, gore signifies a triangular-shaped piece of land. The piece of land next to Gore Lane in Bradwell (called Beggars Plot) is an obvious example, and Ings is simply an Old Norse word for a meadow. Plex or pleckes is a small enclosure as is a pingle, although it may be that the latter is slightly smaller, probably more like a paddock. A close is almost self-explanatory, being an enclosed field, while lea is an arable field or pasture meadow, or a clearing in a wood or area of scrub into which cattle would have been driven for identification or slaughter after being loose on the common.

Hay and hey denote a small field enclosed by a fence, which could be a wooden fence, a hedge or even stone walls, as in its true meaning, 'fence' just means a barrier or defence. One is reminded of an American visitor to the Peak District who commented on the 'stone fences'. Hay appears to be used for an area into which beasts were put, hence names such as Oxhey.

Butts is interpreted by most people as being a place to practise archery, and that is one meaning, presumably when the field would have to be fairly lengthy. Butt is more often a small irregularly shaped piece of land at the boundary of other fields or disjoined from them. Land which has been brought into cultivation, inclosed or 'taken in' from moorland frequently takes the name of intake. Grazing land at the side of a road is sometimes known as 'Long Meadow', and houses built on these places assume the name.

Croft in field names is a small enclosure of pasture or arable land, generally with a cottage in close proximity, and flat(t) speaks for itself. Dole is arable common land that has been allocated to individuals, or the Church as in Church Doles, Cronkston; it was not unusual to carry out this division by drawing lots.

OTHER ANIMALS AND INSECTS

A valuable food source until relatively recently was the rabbit. Rabbits were kept in warrens, and the field name Cunnery (from the old name, coney) is to be found in Outseats, Castleton and Rowsley. The older form Conegry is found at Highlow. It is often said that there are only two words in the English language ending in –gry, i.e. angry and hungry – well, there's another one.

The Urchin Hole in Great Hucklow is named after the hedgehog. Asker Meadow in Bosley was once inhabited by newts, the dialect words of asker and askel still being used in the West Midlands area. A variation of the northern dialect word for a hare, malkin, accounts for the name Mawkin Holes in Macclesfield Forest. To come to the smallest insect with a field named after it, we have a number of cases of Louse or Lousy, which means just what it says – a lice-infected area.

STATE OF THE LAND

The fitness of the land for tilling or crop production has produced a plethora of descriptions of the most imaginative kind. In Brough there is a field called

Betterest, which could be construed as 'better rest', but is a local way of saying the best. The author went to school with a lad whose nickname was Wusser, because when his mother was ill and people enquired about her health his stock reply was 'no worser'.

Back Break Meadow in Smerrill; Sodom in Brampton; Pityful in Bakewell; Bastard Leys in Fenny Bentley; Barren Close in Abney; Meek Fields in Barlow, and Spitewinter all graphically illustrate what the tenant thought of the field.

Again, unproductive land would raise the spectre of poverty, giving rise to such names as Bare Bottoms in Outseats; Bare Arse Pingle in Youlgreave; and a number of field names containing the word 'beggar' or 'beggary' (although this could on occasions refer to beggars in the vicinity), and various fields called Hungry or Hunger Hill.

An older resident of Elton, on being asked the name of a field, said it was 'Ongrill', and it was quite a while before realisation dawned that this is a local pronunciation of Hunger Hill, quite a useful lesson for anyone carrying out oral local history! Place-name expert Dr Reaney advised that the best way to get near to the root meaning and pronunciation of a name was to ask a local whose family have lived there for generations. Which reminds one of the local who imperiously announced that: 'You're not a local until you've had relatives in the churchyard for three hundred years!'

The farmers expressed their opinion of difficulties in working the land with clear description like Sour Lands at Great Hucklow, which would be cold, wet and retaining stagnant moisture, and Dirt Hole in Green Fairfield and similar names which imply muddy or miry ground, although the author's farming relatives used to refer to thistly fields as dirty. Other fields which do not sound enticing are the many containing the word pudding, meaning sticky ground like a pudding, the exception being if a pudding-pie kiln was sited here. There is an affliction from which animals suffer, locally called bellond, which is a form of lead poisoning and so there are fields called Bellond Field in Hathersage, and Bellandy Piece in both Matlock and Walton.

It cannot be clear whether the various fields called Mount Pleasant signify good or bad land, as it is a title often given in a sarcastic way. Loam Close and Butterlands in Wincle; Butter Field in Great Hucklow; Cheeselow Close in Monyash; Paradise in Green Fairfield and in Edale, Fat Close, Cuckoo Butts (an early crop) and the wonderfully-named Sweet Lips in Middleton-by-Youlgreave, all testify to the fertility of their sites.

BIRDS AND BEES

Only very occasionally do birds appear in field names, and Pheasant Pingle in Alderwasley; Partridge Dole, Wessington, and Dove Lands are obvious examples. As the last named is in Tansley there can be no doubt it refers to the bird and not the river. Throstle Nest, Hognaston, refers to the song thrush, while Lopping Sitch alludes to the lapwing or peewit.

In Curbar there is a Bee Croft, and in Chapel-en-le-Frith a Bee Hole Meadow; whether bees were kept in hives or were just found here naturally would require further investigation. Hope, Hathersage, and Parwich all have fields containing the word honey, and the assumption would be that these too were places where bees were kept. However, it could be argued that honey is a complimentary name for good land, or even that it is sticky soil with the consistency of honey

SPORT

Fields called Bowling Alley in Kirk Ireton and Alderwasley, might well have been used for that purpose, or it could be that it is a flat piece of land which would be suitable for the game. In Brackenfield there is a Wrestling Piece which would have been the venue for matches. Cockshut Meadow in Pott Shrigley would previously have been a place to catch woodcock; a cockshut (or cockshoot) is a glade in a wood through which woodcock dart, shoot, or fly, and hunters catch them by stretching a net across the opening to snare the birds.

Hawkesyard in Wincle and Hawksmoor in Hognaston were places where trained hawks were flown to catch small animals and other birds. The name Hawksmoor is also the name of a wood in the Churnet Valley, and this too was a hunting forest owned by the monks of Croxden Abbey.

There is a Plaistow in Crich, pronounced play-stow, and this is where folks met to play. Apparently the car park to Peak Cavern in Castleton is called Jousting Field, and if this is so would no doubt have obvious connections with Peveril Castle and the medieval tournaments which were once held there.

OVER YONDER

Distants in Great Hucklow, Outlands and Outskirts in Edale tell us that they are a fair way from the village, while other field names indicate their remoteness by adopting the names of far-flung places that had been recently discovered and named by the fast-expanding British Empire. Some examples of these are

Philadelphia, Newfoundland, North America, Mount Sinai, Gibraltar, Jericho, China Pasture, Pondicherry (India) and Barbados.

Alma, although in the distant Crimea, is no doubt a celebration of the Battle of the Alma in 1854, when the combined British and French armies defeated the Russians. Scotland occurs quite often and could well be in this category, or it might refer to a Scot, which was a tax on the land and used to benefit the poor of the parish. Such fields are often found on the parish boundary.

MISCELLANEOUS

There are a few notable names that do not appear to fit into the above categories and they are mentioned here. Baulk is found in Hathersage and in Hazlebadge, and is a strip of land left unploughed, whether by design or accident, between furrows or along the boundary of a field. Copyhold Close in Hope signifies ownership by the lord of the manor, with the right of holding land being granted by means of a copy of a roll made by the lord's court. Demesne Land as found in Bonsall also means the land belonged to the lord of the manor, and was retained for his own use as part of the main farm of the manor. Home Farm is a farm attached to or near the most important house in the village.

Demesne is related to domain. Sometimes demesne land is shortened to mesne, as in Mesne Close in both Abney and Curbar, and Mesne Lane in Bakewell. Demesne and Mesne are words not normally encountered, and are pronounced 'di-meen' and 'meen' respectively. Mean Field in Edale, on the other hand, denotes land held in common.

15
WHAT'S INN A NAME?

The Peak District contains a little-noticed but fascinating open-air picture gallery and reminder of times past – the art of the inn sign. Behind the art of the sign and the pub name there is often a story of local or national history, and in this section we will consider just a few.

In Roman days the simple device of a bush displayed in front of the premises denoted a tavern – hence the Hollybush, such as the example at Grangemill at the top of the Via Gellia. Soon the locals knew where to get a decent pint, or a good wine, and didn't need a bush to tell them; hence the saying: 'A good wine needs no bush.'

One of the oldest remaining inn signs in the country, the Eagle and Child on a former inn near Gradbach

Much later, Richard II decreed that all alehouses must display a sign. In deference to him many inns adopted his emblem of a White Hart as their sign. Others used the arms or emblem of the local landowner; The Three Stags Heads, Devonshire Arms, and Snake Inn are examples from the Cavendish family of Chatsworth House; and the Manners and the Peacock at Rowsley, for the owners of Haddon Hall. Incidentally, at the time of writing the sign of the Manners in Bakewell by some quirk displays the arms of the rival Devonshires.

The Wanted Inn at Sparrowpit was once the Devonshire Arms, but it closed and stood empty for many a year. When the Buswell family bought it they changed the name to show that the empty building was indeed now wanted. The Surrey Arms and Norfolk Arms show the influence of the Dukes of Norfolk, especially in the Glossop area.

The wide-ranging estates of the Harpur-Crewe family of Calke Abbey and Warslow Hall are shown in the Crewe and Harpur in Longnor, and the Eyre family of Hassop and Hathersage is also well represented. The Earls of Derby lead to the names Stanley Arms and the Eagle and Eagle and Child.

There is an interesting tale as to how the Eagle and Child crest came about. Sir Thomas Latham, an Earl of Derby in the fourteenth century, sired an illegitimate daughter. He had the child placed under a tree in which an eagle had nested so that he could just 'happen upon' the baby while walking past with his wife. The girl was adopted by them and named Isobel. She subsequently married Sir John Stanley – combining their estates and inheriting a crest.

Various royal names are found on signs, although by law it can never be a living monarch. The Royal Oak recalls Charles II's escape by hiding in the Boscobel Oak in Shropshire after his defeat by Parliamentary forces at Worcester in 1651. After the Restoration his birthday, May 29, was known as Royal Oak Day or Oak Apple Day by way of thanksgiving. Presumably his father's head is in the basket below the executioner's axe on the current King's Head sign in Buxton.

National history and pride is depicted in such as the Battle of Agincourt, when Henry V's army of English archers slew 10,000 Frenchmen on St Crispin's Day, 1415. An interesting account of the battle is given on the wall of the Crispin Inn at Ashover. But the Crispin at Great Longstone is said to take its name from the patron saint of cobblers – because shoemaking and mending was once a thriving village industry.

Four hundred years later, on 18 June, 1815, Wellington's troops had an even bloodier victory over Napoleon at Waterloo when 47,000 men lay dead or injured. By the time of the Crimean Battle of the River Alma in 1854, the French and British were allies who combined to defeat the Russians. Both these battles are remembered in local inn names. Despite being in the centre of the country, well away from the sea, both Nelson and Admiral Jervis, a Staffordshire man whose family owned land in Onecote, are remembered in Peakland pub names.

John Manners, the Marquis of Granby, son of the Duke of Rutland was an eighteenth-century soldier. He was Commander-in-Chief of the British Army and was generous in setting up his former soldiers as publicans, who in turn loyally named their establishments after him. Still on a military note, Frederick Augustus Duke of York, a popular officer because of the reforms he brought about, is frequently pictured on signs.

Some inns are named after topographical features, such as the Winking Man on the A53 between Leek to Buxton near the prominent face-like rock which appears to wink as the motorist travels past it. The Lantern Pike is named after the nearby hill of the same name, and readers of a certain vintage may well remember a popular television series called 'Fabian of the Yard', which was based on a real detective, and it was he who solved the murder of the landlady here in 1927. The other claim to fame of this pub is that Tony Warren hatched the idea of 'Coronation Street' here when it was his local.

The Sir William stands at the bottom of Sir William Hill at Grindleford, and there has been much speculation as to whom the hill was named after. Although it is generally thought to be Sir William Bagshaw (1771–1832), this is highly unlikely. The name appears to have been given to the hill in the seventeenth century, so the main contenders must be either Sir William Cavendish, who lived at nearby Stoke Hall at that time, or Sir William Saville, who was lord of the manor at the time.

However, the Crag Inn at Wildboarclough, in the shadow of Shutlingsloe in Cheshire, doesn't take its name from the shapely summit, but from the former name of the village.

It comes as a surprise to find a pub called The Ship Inn in the Cheshire part of the Peak District. The present sign shows Sir Ernest Shackleton's ship the *Nimrod,* which sailed to the Antarctic in 1907 with local landowner Lieutenant Colonel Sir Philip Brocklehurst as a member of the crew. The original ship was the *Sweet Emily* owned by Messrs Moore & Co, which was lost near the Cape on 31 August, 1861. The ship was actually called the *Swythamley,* but the sailors supposedly had difficulty pronouncing that name and rechristened her.

Industries of the past are recalled by the Millstone at Hathersage, and the Miners' Standard above Winster. Strangers to the area could be forgiven for thinking the last mentioned to be a flag, but the standard refers to the standard dish used to measure lead ore.

A reminder of Matlock Bath's and Bradwell's attempts to attract spa patronage in an age when hydrotherapy was all the rage is the New Bath, and although the Scotsman's Pack could refer to a gent from north of the border, it almost certainly got its name from a 'Scotchman', which is an old name for an itinerant trader, often a linen trader. A previous sign spelled the name of the inn as Scotchman's Pack.

For many years the only way to transport goods was by packhorse, and this common pub name is to be found near old trade routes, such as the Packhorse at Little Longstone. Later transportation systems which gave their names to pubs were the Navigation or canal, and the Railway. The railway companies also gave their names to pubs, such as The Midland at Matlock Bath.

The Greyhound at Warslow was apparently named after a local stagecoach, and the Setter Dog, which is situated on the Buxton to Macclesfield turnpike, could have taken its name from the slang term for a lookout or the highwayman's accomplice who would spy the coaches and travellers coming over the hills.

One of the many signs with a religious origin is the Cross Keys, referring to St Peter, the keeper of the keys to Heaven. Another is the Anchor and the Hope and Anchor, which are taken from St Paul's words: 'We have this as a sure and steadfast anchor of the soul, a hope...' The Bull, and Bull's Head are often to be found near a church and some say the origin of these signs is the papal bull, which is a lead seal authenticating edicts from the Pope.

Some sporting signs of interest in the Peak District are the unusually named Flying Childers, which was a famous racehorse trained by a Mr Childers for the Duke of Devonshire. Perhaps the grateful innkeeper had put some money on it. The Sportsman at Hayfield no doubt refers to the local sport of game shooting, and we also have the Grouse. The Grouse and Claret at Rowsley, however, has an angling connection, being the favourite fishing fly of a local water bailiff. Angling also features in the Charles Cotton, as this Hartington man was a great friend of Izaak Walton and contributed a chapter to Walton's classic fishing bible, *The Compleat Angler*.

The fascinating caves, seats, and steps at Rowter Rocks were carved out in the early nineteenth century, but the suggestion was that it was the ancient druids who had created them, and the nearby Druid Inn adopted a suitable name. At one time they even had a guide to escort visitors around the site.

Two oddities are the pictures on the signs of the Duke of York at Pomeroy on the A515 Ashbourne–Buxton road, which shows Richard III, who was Duke of Gloucester; and the Miners Arms at Carsington which paradoxically depicts a coal miner and headstock, in what was predominantly a lead mining area.

One inn that virtually all visitors to the Peak District know is the Cat and Fiddle. It is a well-known landmark sitting on the heather moorland high above the Goyt Valley on the A537 Buxton–Macclesfield road at an altitude of 1690 feet (515m). This makes it the second highest pub in England. Incidentally, as it is just in Cheshire it isn't, as is sometimes heard, the highest inn in Derbyshire, so that honour goes to The Barrel at Bretton.

So how did it come by its name? Once again, nobody really knows, but there are various explanations from which to take your pick. The pub was built by a Macclesfield banker called John Ryle in 1831, but this inn name has been popular since the early sixteenth century, so it could simply be a name that he fancied.

Other explanations are that the Duke of Devonshire gave the owner a picture of a cat and fiddle; the Duke liked to drive up here with a cat and a fiddle for solitude; or that it was named after an English knight called Caton who held Calais, and was called Caton Fidele.

Probably, all of these are highly unlikely, especially the last as the sign had appeared elsewhere before Caton existed. If the truth is known, it was probably just a jolly sign taken from the popular nursery rhyme, 'Hey Diddle Diddle, the Cat and the Fiddle.'

No explanation seems to exist for the unique name The Flouch Inn, near Langsett. It is a name which defies etymologists, the best guess being that it was once The Plough and the tail fell off the 'g' and then the loop of the 'P' wore off on the right-hand side.

A glance at old directories will show that all villages had a plethora of pubs in the last century, and they continue to dwindle. If one looks at the history of public houses, it will be found that name changes are quite common. This is still happening, but recently with a much reduced momentum.

Two examples were given names taken from the stories of J.R.R. Tolkein, The Hobbit at Monyash, and The Prancing Pony in Eyam. The Hobbit has now reverted to its former name of the Bull's Head, and the other, which was the Royal Oak, is a now private residence. Another Bull's Head which has gone back to its original title is the one at Foolow, which for a spell was The Lazy Landlord. The Wetherspoon chain has opened two establishments in the Peak, the Crown in Matlock retaining its name, and the former Ashwood in Buxton taking the name Wye House, presumably because of its proximity to the River Wye, although a previous building in town with that name was the lunatic asylum.

Finally, it does seem that pub landlords can be particularly unfortunate in their choice of spouse. One of the most famous inn signs in the Peak District is the Quiet Woman at Earl Sterndale, above the Upper Dove Valley. The sign, which depicts a headless woman, a device found in other parts of the country including Leek, is supposed to represent a wife nicknamed 'Chattering Charteris', whose constant nagging eventually drove her husband to decapitate her. The sentiment expressed on the sign, 'Soft words turneth away wrath,' was obviously not enough to save her!

The Quiet Woman at Earl Sterndale – how long will this sign exist in these politically correct days?

16
UNDERGROUND NOMENCLATURE

The limestone part of the Peak District is riddled with caves, caverns, and underground passages carved out by water many years ago. Four of the best known are found in Castleton.

Peak Cavern has one of the largest natural cave entrances in Europe and sports a most prosaic name given by the Victorians who objected to the previous one, the Devil's Arse. Presumably this was thought to be an exit from Hell. There is a folk tale of a goose flying into Eldon Hole and re-emerging from Peak Cavern some days later with singed wings. In the last few years, the cavern has been advertised using its old name, not to everyone's taste, but visitor numbers have apparently increased.

Blue John Cavern is so-called because of the rare, semi-precious stone which has been mined here. Blue John presumably gained its title from the days when the Peverils held sway in the High Peak, as it is reputedly from the French description of its blue and yellow colours, *bleu jaune*. It is a form of banded fluorspar which gets its colour from dissolved petroleum.

Treak Cliff is an interesting name; Treak is interpreted as 'pain, affliction, or grief' with 'oak', and the assumption is that this means that criminals were hanged here. However, oak trees were revered by the ancients and were thought to imbue people who visited them with the strength and courage to carry on, and this would apply to those suffering grief or pain. Speedwell is a cave much extended in a fruitless attempt at lead mining and like so many mines has a fanciful name, in this case that of a pretty little wild flower.

In Buxton there is a spectacular cave open to the public called Poole's Cavern. Poole was according to legend an outlaw in the fifteenth century, and 'proof' of this is the fact that three silver coins bearing the head of Henry VI who was crowned in 1431. In 1636 Thomas Hobbes wrote his *De Mirabilis Pecci*, or 'Wonders of the Peak' in which he included Poole's Hole, and tells us that Poole was a famous thief equal to Caccuss and 'perchance as old'. A few years later, in 1681, Ralph Thoresby wrote of 'Pool (sic) of Pool's Hall in Staffordshire, a man of great valour who, being outlawed, resided here for his own security'.

Bagshaw Cavern in Bradwell, which is an ideal 'starter' for aspiring potholers, was discovered by lead miners in 1806, and they named it after Lady Bagshawe of Wormhill Hall. When the cave had been made more accessible, some quarter of a century later, she visited the cave and named all the various shapes and openings she saw.

There is a cave in Deep Dale near Chelmorton called Thirst House, which no doubt has a story attached to it, as it means 'giant's house'. The hamlet of Malcoff means 'bad or dangerous pothole or cave', but exactly where this is the author has not determined.

This section ends with a trawl through the amazing names of caves, potholes, and lead mines and lists some of the most intriguing – with few exceptions, there is no explanation of the origin of the name given them by their discoverers.

Beans and Bacon; Blobber; Bald Mare; Black Rabbit Cave; Boggard; Blobber; Clear the Way; Cowslop; Crash Purse; Critchlow Cave (in times of heavy rain or thawing snow, water pours from this cave which is on the opposite side of the dale to Lathkill Head Cave, the usual source of the River Lathkill, to create a veritable torrent); Daily Bread; Dr Jackson's Cave; Etches Cave (a Mr Etches lives at nearby Dowel Hall Farm); Fiery Dragon; Giant's Hole, Golconda; Good Luck Mine; Hang Worm; Have at All; Ladywash; Lickpenny (this is an obsolete word for stinginess or something which is a drain on the purse, and suggests that the mine was not very productive); Lucky Ploughman; Merlin's Mine; Nettle Pot (named by Walter Sissons who found the pothole when his dog chased a rabbit through nettles, in the process dislodging stones at the entrance); Nimblejack; Old Isaac's Venture; Perseverance; Prince Charles; St Bertram's Cave; Silence; Smiling Fancy; Suckstone; Suicide Cave; Tearbreeches, and to finish, perhaps what you most need after a caving trip, Warm Bath.

17

ON THE RIGHT TRACK

Roads, tracks or pathways in place-names can throw up some fascinating information. Given the well-known Peak weather, some roads were only usable in good weather, so we come across names like Summer Lane, at Wirksworth.

It is a generally known fact that 'gate' in the Peak means road or path, from the Old Norwegian 'gata', a way. Examples are Chapel Gate – the way to Chapel-en-le-Frith; Cutgate – was Cart Gate in 1574; Castle Gate and Siggate ('side-gate') – the road to Peveril Castle; Burgate – the road to the fortified place, and Batham Gate – the way to the warm chalybeate baths in Buxton. Incidentally, there are some weird and wonderful pronunciations of chalybeate which is properly kal-ib-ee-ate.

Leisure Farm near Litton Slack stands at the end of a way that was known in 1764 as Leisure Gate and meaning the way to the meadow. Chesterfield has some interesting street names incorporating 'gate'. But a word of warning: it is easy to draw the wrong conclusions by taking odd names off a map. Kinder Gates is nothing to do with roadways, but rather a natural rock formation through which the infant River Kinder flows.

Knifesmithgate in Chesterfield does not come from the cutlery trade, but is a family name, while Glumangate has no connection with glue makers, but means the street of the minstrel, Gleeman being an old word for a minstrel. Saltergate, where the local football team has its home ground, indicates the route taken by the packhorse trains carrying their valuable cargo of salt from the Cheshire 'wiches'.

The routes, or salt ways, taken by these transporters can be traced on a map by such names as Salterbrook, Salterford, Salter's Knowl, Saltersich, and Jaggers Lane. Field names give an indication of ways, paths, or roads passing through them or close to them, and in this context we have Saltersford in Tideswell and Saltersway in Chelmorton, clearly being on the route of a saltway from Cheshire.

The man in charge of the packhorse train was called a jagger. Whether this name comes from the breed of horses, Jaeger (although Galloways were a popular choice), or because they carried loads, jags in dialect, is not really known. Incidentally, tracing routes by names cannot be an exact science, for example Jagger's Clough on Kinder Scout does not have any known packhorse way passing through it, and it probably takes its name from a someone with the surname Jagger.

Packhorse travel has left its mark in place-names; according to this sign in Hayfield it is 4 miles over the hills to Glossop

80

In the infant River Dane at Three Shires Head near Galleywood Bridge is a deep pond called Panniers Pool, named after the pannier or basket slung on each side of the packhorse to carry the load. As it stands near the junction of a number of packhorse ways it does not stretch the imagination too much to see that it was called after them by the jaggers who passed this way. The route from Edale to Hayfield, now incorporating Jacobs' Ladder, was in 1609 known as Old Horse Waie.

Street, stret, and strat in place-names invariably imply that it stands on or near a Roman Road. Street Farm at Pomeroy sits on the Roman road simply known as The Street which ran from Little Chester (Derby) to *Aqua Arnemetiae* (Buxton). The same road passed a field called Over Street near Flagg and Straight Knolls Barn in Brassington, which was Streetknowle in 1620, meaning the hillock by the street.

Mouldridge, near Pikehall, has been interpreted as the 'raised Roman road by a hill'. Stretfield Road and Causeway Meadow, Bradwell, stand on Batham Gate, the way from the Roman fort at *Navio* to Buxton, a fact acknowledged by one of the house-names, 'Cohorts Way'. A causeway or causey is a raised road of stone flags over soft ground.

Navio is at the place now called Brough, which means a Roman fortification. The Street in South Wingfield means the nearby Roman road, Ryknield Way.

Load is an old word for a path or way, and this is the probable meaning of Loads near Holymoorside, although it can mean a stream. There is also a Longload Lane in Middleton-by-Wirksworth, and Lamaload means a loamy track. Load or lode can also be a watercourse, so there is always an element of doubt about the name. Lode Mill near Milldale could fall into either category.

It is often stated that Doctor's Gate at Glossop is a Roman road. It is true that one does run very close by, but the line is slightly away from this path. Doctor's Gate was probably a very old route which was later named after Dr Talbot, an illegitimate son of the Earl of Shrewsbury. He was appointed vicar of Glossop and paved the track across the moors towards his family seat in Sheffield in the late fifteenth century.

One could be forgiven for thinking that the Via Gellia road (A5012) has Roman origins. It does not. It was created by Philip Gell of Hopton Hall in 1791–92 from his lead mines to connect with Cromford canal wharf. The Gells claimed Roman forebears, having found a slab in 1792 bearing the inscription *GELL PRAE C III LV BRIT;* hence the rather grand name for this road. The slab is apparently now lost.

It is worth mentioning here that the trade name for the fabric called Viyella is inspired by Via Gellia, as the manufacturers, Coats & Co, had a mill here. As the mill was a garnetting mill for heavy woollen cloth it is pretty safe to assume that Viyella was not actually made here.

Although 'road' is a common enough word now it doesn't appear to have been much used before the sixteenth century. Gate, lane, and way were the most usual designations. Indeed, we still have the wayside and the highway, and still ask: 'Do you know the way?' Windyway House near Teggs Nose takes its name from the nearby Buxton-to-Macclesfield 'Stoneyway' road which was also known, no doubt appropriately, as the Windyway. Hollow Way, or Holloway, is an ancient way so-called because the constant tramping of man and beast has worn away the ground, eventually making a sunken, or hollow, path or track.

Two bridges leading from the county of Derby into neighbouring counties are Derbyshire Bridge, heading for Cheshire from the Goyt Valley, and Yorkshire Bridge, heading for Yorkshire from the Upper Derwent Valley above Bamford. Whaley Bridge was called Whaley, (pronounced waylee) meaning 'clearing by the road', and the bridge part was added later.

The packhorse bridge in Milldale, Viator's Bridge, gains its name from being mentioned in Izaak Walton's classic book on fishing, *The Compleat Angler.* The main characters in the book are Piscator the fisherman, based on the author, Izaak Walton, and Viator the traveller, based on his friend Charles Cotton from Hartington. Viator is not impressed with the dimensions of the bridge and declares that it: "Tis but two fingers broad and a mouse can hardly go over it.'

Lidgate near Chapel-en-le-Frith, also to be found near Holmesfield, and Lydgate at Bamford, and Blackwell, all mark the places where a swing gate blocked the road to stop cattle straying. The noisy-sounding Clatterway in Bonsall is said to get its name from the noise made by loose stones: clater in Old English. Rumbling Street is also supposedly named after the rumble of traffic, although this is harder to swallow as the name is recorded as long ago as 1668. Was seventeenth century traffic so loud?

The Portway is an ancient road leading to a 'port' or market town. It runs across the Peak District from the direction of Belper and heading roughly northwest towards Castleton. It passes through Alport Height, Portaway Mine near Elton, Alport hamlet, then through Ashford-in-the-Water to continue along Castlegate Lane to Castleton.

A clue that this ancient road passed close by is given by the field name of Portaway, in Carsington; in the same area there is a Wayland Bit, and a Wayland Close, which have no relationship to Wayland the Smith but mean land by the path, or way. Could this be the same path taken by the packhorses led by the man who gave his name to yet another nearby field called Jaggers Way?

In Wessington, The Driftway gets its name from the old word for a cattle road, drift, plus way. Stoop Close in Abney also suggests that a road came this way and travellers were guided by the stoop, or guidepost, sited there, as they were in Guide Post Field near Eyam. Following various acts of Parliament dating from 1702, parishes were compelled to erect posts or stoops as they are called locally, at critical places such as crossroads, to direct travellers to the next market town.

Brierlow Bar is the site of the toll-bar which came with the turnpike road of 1773. A bar was sometimes precisely that – a pivoted bar of wood or iron placed across the road to ensure that no one avoided paying the toll. However, 'bar' as in Baslow Bar means a 'horseway leading up a steep hill', and Bargate also means the steep road.

The Snake Path and the Snake Road owe nothing to their tortuous routes, but take their name, as does the Snake Inn, from the knowed (knotted to you and me) serpent of the Devonshire family's coat of arms.

Weaddow Lane is thought to mean the 'weather way' or 'sheltered way', while Twitchill at Hope means the 'narrow footpath'. A wall on Meadow Lane between Tideswell and Millers Dale incorporates the base of the fifteenth-century Butterton Cross. Clearly this is nowhere near Butterton, and the explanation is that the previous name of this lane was Butterton Lane. Thomas Meverell who was the local lord of the manor also held land in Butterton, and transferred the name to this road.

18
SO THE STORY GOES...

There are many places in the Peak District with a story, whether true or not, behind the name. This last chapter is devoted to some of the more interesting stories and legends attached to some of them.

White Nancy is, as the name implies, normally painted white, but Christmas is a special time of year

The original Clod Hall, on East Moor near Baslow, was supposedly a clod hovel, a clod being a lump of turf, which was built by one William Kay. He had smoke issuing from its chimney within twenty-four hours of its erection, thus claiming the land and building. Black Harry Gate near Stoney Middleton is said to be named after a highwayman. This was his 'patch', and the story goes that he was eventually caught and hanged at Wardlow Mires.

Flash village had a cottage industry of button making, connected to the silk mills in Leek, and it is said that the machines were also used to counterfeit coins. These coins were known as flash money. Flash language was a slang spoken by thieves, and this too supposedly originated from this village; there is even an entry to this effect in the *Oxford English Dictionary*. A flashman is a pedlar, and Flash village was a centre for such people, travelling in buttons and silk ribbons, in the 1700s. The more mundane explanation of Flash is a pool or marshy place.

The three cairns on Gardom's Edge known as The Three Men are in remembrance of three inebriated clergymen who became lost in the snow here after attending a funeral in Eyam, according to one version of the tale.

The monument called White Nancy standing on the Ridge of Kerridge, above Bollington, is shown on older maps as Northern Nancy. It originally had a door and was used as a summerhouse, and was erected in 1817 to celebrate Wellington's victory over Napoleon's army at Waterloo two years previously.

There are conflicting stories of the nomenclature. There is a large circular stone slab inside the building which was pulled up the hill by eight horses, one of which was called Nancy. On the other hand, the family responsible for erecting the structure lived at Ingersley Hall, near Rainow, and they had a daughter of that name.

It is commonly put about that the Roosdyche (pronounced roos-dike) near Chinley was created as a Roman raceway. There is no evidence for this and any competent geologist could explain how it was formed, probably by meltwater under a glacier. It means 'hollow or ditch on the moor'.

There are at least four Lovers' Leaps in the Peak District, each, no doubt, with its unique tale to tell. The one off Ashwood Dale in Buxton was leapt over by two eloping lovers on one horse, the speed enabling the animal to clear the chasm. They apparently managed to reach the Gretna Green of the Peak at Peak Forest and married before the pursuant parents arrived. The Lovers' Leap in

Stoney Middleton harks back to 1760 when a jilted and heartbroken young woman called Hannah Baddaley jumped off the cliff. But her voluminous petticoats billowed out when she fell, acting like a parachute, and she survived to reach a ripe old age.

A leap of the unintentional kind was made by the vicar of Monyash, the Revd Lomas, in about 1776. He was allegedly in an inebriated state whilst riding his horse back to the village, and inadvertently fell off a cliff into Lathkill Dale, breaking his neck. The cliff is now called Parson's Tor.

Little John, faithful lieutenant of the outlaw Robin Hood, is reputedly buried in Hathersage churchyard near to where he was born, and there is a pub named after him in the village, in addition to a well on the National Trust's nearby Longshaw estate.

Robin Hood is well represented in place-names; there is the Robin Hood Inn and hamlet above Baslow, a well, caves on Stanage Edge, climbing routes, a stoop, and Robin Hood's Picking Rods. The last named are the base and shafts of a double cross-boundary marker for the lands of Basingwerk Abbey. Popular folklore has it that 'picking' was carried out here, especially the picking a wife. They had an earlier name of the Maiden Stones.

The Bow Stones above Lyme Park are strikingly similar, and both sets of stones are commonly believed to have been used to bend and string bows. Robin Hood's Stoop on the Stanage moors is probably the remains of a medieval cross. Local mythology tells us that Robin shot an arrow from here into Hathersage churchyard, where there is a not dissimilar pillar. The distance is 1¼ miles! The longest distance attained by an arrow from a long-bow is otherwise thought to be 344 yards, achieved by Sir Ralph Payne-Galway in 1906 at Norton Priory.

Dollwood Tor or Mock Beggar's Hall, near Elton, is nowadays better known as Robin Hood's Stride. Legend tells us that this gentleman could stride the gap between the pinnacles of Inaccessible and Weasel, a mere 70 feet (21m).

But that is small beer to the man who gave his name to the rock on Bosley Cloud known as Giant's Shoe. He stood here with his other foot on top of Shutlingsloe! Another giant called Aigle is said to be responsible for hurling the huge boulder, the Aigle or Eagle Stone, to its present location on Baslow Moor.

People in Onecote village, pronounced 'on-cut', will tell you that when Bonnie

Robin Hood's Picking Rods, the remains of a double cross-boundary marker erected by the monks of Basingwerk Abbey

Prince Charlie's men passed this way, they considered Onecote not worth bothering with, as there was not even a warm winter coat to steal. It does, of course, mean 'one cottage', and the name was recorded as long ago as 1199.

The Royal Cottage public house in the Staffordshire Moorlands also has connections with the Young Pretender. He is said to have stayed here during his foray into England in 1745, giving the inn its name. Another incident during the retreat of the highlanders took place on 10 December 1745 at Bosley Cloud. A rifleman shot and killed a drummer boy at the place now called Drummer's Knob.

The boulders below Derwent Edge known as Lost Lad mark the spot where the body of shepherd boy Abraham Lowe was found. He had perished in the snow, after scratching the words 'lost lad' on the rock to aid people searching for him.

There are two ponds called Mermaid Pool in the Peak District, one at Morridge and one on the western slopes of Kinder Scout above Hayfield. They both have their individual legend. You may well think it odd to find reference to a mermaid so far inland, and one suspects it is a corruption of mere-maid. The mermaid said to inhabit the Kinder pool is apparently benign, and anyone who sees her on Easter Eve is guaranteed a long life. The mermaid of Mermaid's Pool on Morridge, otherwise known as Blake Mere, is more sinister. She allegedly lures unsuspecting travellers to their death in the 'unfathomable pit'.

A woman who lived in the seventeenth century and went under the soubriquet of 'the Witch of the Frith' lived by Old Hag Farm. She had the odd habit of transforming herself into a hare for suitable remuneration and allowing herself to be chased by hounds.

The house near Hayfield shown on maps as Highgate is otherwise known as Boggart House. It has, the story goes, a sealed well which if opened will release the boggart which is trapped within. A boggart is a spirit that haunts places where a violent incident has taken place, in this instance the murder of a Scottish pedlar. Terror Bridge near Tunstead House in Hayfield apparently got its name from the incident in the 1800s when a girl was thrown off the horse she was riding and killed.

It is popular mythology that two men were walking near Abney; one of them was cross-eyed, or cock-eyed. They managed to walk into each other and the cock-eyed man said, 'Why don't you look where you're going?', to which the other retorted, 'And why don't you walk where you're looking!' The place where this incident supposedly happened became Cockey Farm.

The street name 'Will Shore's Lane' at Oker near Darley Dale, reminds us of a story concerning this local man. Peter and Will Shore were two brothers from Oker. Peter decided that a brave new world of riches awaited him overseas. For whatever reason, the two brothers each planted a sycamore tree on Oker Hill – some versions of the story say it was for their coffins.

In the event Peter died shortly after emigrating, and his tree also failed to thrive and died. It is said that the prominent sycamore tree still standing on the hill is the one Will planted. This story must have reached the ears of no lesser person than William Wordsworth, for in 1829 he penned the poem about it entitled 'A Tradition of Oker Hill in Darley Dale, Derbyshire'.

The most usual story regarding the Nine Ladies in the Bronze Age stone circle of that name on Stanton Moor, tells us that they were dancing in a most unbecoming manner on the Sabbath. As a result of this misconduct they were turned to stone where they stood, as was the fiddler who became the nearby King Stone. This is a common legend associated with other stone circles throughout the country.

The Nine Ladies, allegedly turned to stone after dancing on the Sabbath

The popular story of how Gladwin's Mark got its name is that a man named Gladwin managed to get lost here in the December snows. In order to keep warm and awake he set about building a cairn and then pulling it down again, and building it up again and again until he was rescued.

Another legend, believed to be true by a great many people, concerns Win Hill and the adjacent Lose Hill. The tale is that the forces of Edwin, King of Northumbria camped on Win Hill before doing battle with the army of Cuicholm, King of Wessex, who were gathered on Lose Hill. The names of the hills tell us who won, despite Lose being pronounced 'loose'.

In 1636 a man from Wormhill was found, with his throat cut by robbers, in Earnshaw Clough near Cutthroat Bridge on the A57 Snake Road on the Sheffield side of Ladybower. He died some days later at the house he was taken to in Bamford, but the bloody incident is forever perpetuated in the place-name.

Bill o' Jacks Plantation, near Dove Stones, is named after Bill Bradbury whose nickname it was. He was both the landlord of a local pub and a gamekeeper. In 1832 he and his son Thomas were found murdered, almost certainly by

Ravensdale Cottages, unkindly dubbed 'Bury-me-Wick' by the Manchester mill workers who lived there

poachers against whom he was due to testify in court. The suspected perpetrators of the crime were found not guilty due to lack of evidence.

There is an idyllic looking street of houses below Cressbrook called Ravensdale Cottages which were built by McConnel & Co., the owners of Cressbrook Mill and estate, in the 1830s. It was apparently not such a romantic place to live for the workforce brought in from Manchester who must have thought it 'back of beyond' compared to their original home, and so nicknamed it Bury-me-Wick, which translates as 'bury me alive'.

It is highly unlikely that places including the words gib, gibb or hanging, have any connection with execution, however, there are some place-names that definitely do. Galleywood Bridge, otherwise known as Three Shires Bridge, near Flash, and Galley Acres field in Bakewell both refer to gallows, as does the more straightforward Gallows Knoll in Hopton.

It was quite usual for a manor to have its own gallows to execute felons, even for what nowadays would be considered minor infringements of the law. One wonders how often use was made of these gallows, and it is a sobering thought that the gruesome 'spectator sport' of public hanging was not abolished until 1868.

There is a record for the Gallows Yard, in Taxal, where the Downes family had the right to hang people within their bailiwick of the Macclesfield Forest. Gautries Hill in Peak Forest probably served an equivalent purpose as it was 'Gallow-trees ' in 1617. Another place of execution was Dethick, which has the sinister meaning of 'death oak'.

Gallows and gibbets were generally on parish boundaries or near crossroads, and it was the practice to bury hanged men, and those who had committed suicide, at crossroads.

Gibbet Field in Wardlow Mires is one such field, and the nearby Peter's Stone has the alternative name of Gibbet Rock. It was here that the body of young Antony Lingard was hung in chains after he was hanged for the murder of the local toll-house keeper. Treak (Cliff), first recorded as Trayoc in 1285, is the 'oak of pain and suffering', which is taken to mean the tree where miscreants were hanged. Killhill in Hope on the other hand in merely a hill which had a kill or kiln on it.

There are one or two other places worth mentioning which don't easily fit into any other category, and some are mentioned here.

On the way between Hayfield and Glossop is a house which used to be shown on maps as Hill's House, but is now acknowledged as Peep o' Day. When Mr Goddard built the house he included an east-facing window in the shape of an eye, which caught the first rays of the rising sun, hence the name.

Melandra Castle is the Roman fort at Glossop, but this is a name invented, it is thought, by a Stockport clergyman and antiquarian as the name didn't appear until 1772. The Roman names for it were Ardotalia, Zerdotalia, or Erdotalia, the last name clearly related to the River Etherow.

Here's where the amateur etymologist, like the author, can have fun trying to work out how Melandra was come by. Was it an anagram of Alderman, or for some obscure reason, Greek for black man?

There are a number of boulders or stones on the high Dark Peak moors with some weird and wonderful names, and here are the reasons for a handful of them. The rocks on Kinder Scout's southern edge known as Ringing Roger are supposedly the 'echoing rocks'. The Wheel Stones on Derwent Edge are also known as the Coach and Horses, and it is plain to see why when viewed from a distance, as it looks like a carriage is being pulled along the edge. Hurkling Stones, on the same edge, take a dialect word to shrug up one's back, as these rocks appear to be doing. There is also an old word 'cluther' meaning a pile or heap which is the reason for the name Cluther Rocks on Kinder Scout.

A visit to the collections of rocks in the Dark Peak called the Salt Cellar and Cakes of Bread on Derwent Edge, and the Boxing Gloves, Woolpacks, and Pagoda on Kinder Scout is all that's needed to see why they are so-called. The Woolpacks on Kinder is also sometimes called Whipsnade or the Mushroom Garden, because of the organic shapes that can be imagined there. Shepherds' Meeting Stones on the Howden Moors was apparently the place where shepherds met to exchange stray sheep. Noe Stool on Kinder is also called the Anvil Stone, as it resembles a blacksmith's anvil, and there are other Anvil Stones to be found on Bleaklow.

Chinley Churn is claimed to be named from the shape being like a milk churn, though not everyone agrees. The other suggestion is that it is 'Kinla's Cairn', whoever Kinla was, but this doesn't fit with the meaning of Chinley which is 'the clearing in the deep valley'.

If viewed from a certain angle, such as the Cat and Fiddle road, Shutlingsloe resembles a famous mountain earning it the soubriquet 'the Cheshire

Matterhorn'. Folks with a similarly good imagination like to designate outcrops of rock as 'castles', for example, Alport Castles on the southern edge of Bleaklow, and the silhouette of Robin Hood's Stride in the dusk gives rise to its alternative name of 'Mock Beggars' Hall'.

Another place-name poser is Bottom o' the Oven in Macclesfield Forest. Perhaps a clue is given by the situation being at the bottom of a valley, and one of the roads being called Oven House Lane.

There is a Spital Bridge in Castleton, and Spital Acres in Tideswell, and both these relate to 'hospital'. The one at Castleton was recorded as 'le hospital de Castilton' in 1373, and was initially a leper hospital, later becoming a charitable institution for the poor, aged, and infirm, before being suppressed in 1548.

Glutton — was this the nickname of someone who ate to excess? No slur implied to Terry Bettney who is only posing for the photograph

This little excursion into Peak District place-names ends with a few personal favourites. I have no explanation for Tiddlybumps Wood in Buxton, and Glutton may be the nickname of some long-forgotten, perhaps greedy, chap. The cuddly sounding Dumkins unfortunately means a cesspit or privy, and the descriptive Featherbed Moss is soft, sometimes very soft, peat bog underfoot. Moss is just another word for bog.

Whenever I visit Ashbourne I wonder just what went on in Dig Street. It was known as Lovedich in 1276 and was perhaps the favoured place for a bit of canoodling?

I very much hope you found this slim volume has whetted your appetite to find out more, and I only regret that it was not possible to include all the interesting place-names to be found in this wonderful area we call the Peak.

BIBLIOGRAPHY

Addy, Sidney Oldall – *A Glossary of Words Used in the Neighbourhood of Sheffield* (1888) reprinted 1998 by Llanerch Publishers

Ball, Harry – *Place-Names in the Moorlands* – Self published

Bate, Keith – *The Many Dales of Derbyshire* (1998) – Self published

Bollington Festival Committee – *When Nancy Was Young...* (Bollington, 1974)

Brumhead, Derek – *New Mills 1894–1994* (New Mills, 1994) – New Mills Town Council

Burt, R. Atkinson, M. Waite, Burnley, R., *The Derbyshire Mineral Statistics 1845–1913* (reprinted 1981)

Burton, I.E., *The Royal Forest of Peak* (Bakewell, 1966), Peak Park Planning Board

Cameron, K., *The Place Names of Derbyshire,* three vols (1959), EPNS

Davies, Peggy, *The Annals of Glossop* (Chinley, 1999), High Peak Borough Council

Dodgson, J.McN., *The Place Names of Cheshire* (1970), EPNS

Farey, John Sen., *General View of the Agriculture and Minerals of Derbyshire Vol 1* (1811) reprinted 1989 by Peak District Mines Historical Society

Field, John, *A History of English Field Names* (1993), Longman

Field, John, *English Field Names* (Gloucester, 1989), Alan Sutton

Ford, Trevor D. & Rieuwerts J.H., *Lead Mining in the Peak District* (Bakewell, 1975), Peak District Mines Historical Society/Peak Park Joint Planning Board

Gelling, Margaret, *Place-names in the Landscape* (1984), Dent

Gelling, Margaret & Cole, Ann, *The Landscape of Place-names* (Stamford, 2000), Shaun Tyas

Griffiths, Bill, *A User-Friendly Dictionary of Old English* (1993), Albion Press

Harris, Helen, *Industrial Archaeology of the Peak District* (Newton Abbot, 1971) David & Charles

Hart, Clive, *North Derbyshire Archaelogical Survey* (Chesterfield, 1984), Derbyshire Archaeological Society

Heaf, Eric, *Tideswell Tracks* (1999), Self published

Hey, David, *Oxford Companion to Local and Family History* (1996), OUP

MacLennan, Malcolm, *Gaelic Dictionary* (1925), reprinted 1979 by Acair Mercat

McMeeken, Louis, *Place-names of the Peak District* (1998), Self published

Mellor, George, *Walks with George* (Hollinsclough, 1996), Hollinsclough Methodist Publications

Nelthorpe, T., *Kinder Log* (Milnthorpe, 1987), Cicerone Press

Pickford, Doug, *Myths and Legends of East Cheshire and the Moorlands* (Wilmslow, 1992), Sigma Press

Richardson, John, *The Local Historian's Encyclopedia* (1986), Historical Publications

Rieuwerts, J.H., *Glossary of Derbyshire Lead Mining Terms* (Matlock, 1998), Peak District Mines Historical Society

Turbutt, Gladwyn, *A History of Derbyshire* (1999), Merton Priory Press